ETHNICITY AND EVERYDAY LIFE

Mixing theories of the everyday with a wide range of case studies, this book explains the 'character' of ethnicity, from being a political tool of exclusion, to a source of meaning and solidarity, and the relationship between culture, power and identity.

Combining theories of the everyday with empirical case studies, this book examines:

- the 'dual character' of ethnicity – as a political tool of exclusion and source of meaning/ solidarity respectively;
- the relationship between culture, power, and identity;
- the significance of historical/ socio-economic contexts to ethnicity and everyday life.

What is the relationship between culture and ethnicity? What is sociology's contribution to the interdisciplinary study of everyday ethnicity? How are ethnic groups constructed and encroached upon by (external) power structures? Do ethnic groups resist? How are power and agency exercised within ethnic communities? How do migration, 'diaspora-living' and marginalization affect people's sense of self? How do 'ethnic majorities' negotiate their dominant national identities in everyday life? How might 'identity' and its relation to cultural ideas and practices be conceptualized? What is the significance of everyday ethnicity among asylum seekers and host-populations in an era of globalization? This book addresses these important questions through a critical application of theories of the everyday to a series of case studies that include Travellers, the South Asian diaspora, contemporary Austria, and asylum seekers in 'Fortress Europe'.

This book will provide an accessible and coherent introduction to the sociology of ethnicity and will be essential reading for undergraduate students on cultural studies, race and ethnic studies, and sociology courses.

Christian Karner is a Lecturer in the School of Sociology and Social Policy at the University of Nottingham. His research centres on ethnicity, national identities, and religion. His publications include *The Thought World of Hindu Nationalism: Analyzing a Political Ideology* (2006) and *Writing History, Constructing Religion* (2005, co-edited with J. Crossley).

THE NEW SOCIOLOGY

Series Editor: ANTHONY ELLIOTT, Flinders University, Australia

The New Sociology is a book series designed to introduce students to new issues and themes in social sciences today. What makes the series distinctive, as compared to other competing introductory textbooks, is a strong emphasis not just on key concepts and ideas but on how these play out in everyday life – on how theories and concepts are lived at the level of selfhood and cultural identities, how they are embedded in interpersonal relationships, and how they are shaped by, and shape, broader social processes.

Forthcoming in the series:

Religion and Everyday Life
STEPHEN HUNT (2005)

Culture and Everyday Life
DAVID INGLIS (2005)

Community and Everyday Life
GRAHAM DAY (2005)

Self-Identity and Everyday Life
HARVIE FERGUSON (2005)

Consumption and Everyday Life
MARK W. D. PATERSON (2005)

Globalization and Everyday Life
LARRY RAY (2006)

The Body and Everyday Life
HELEN THOMAS (2006)

Nationalism and Everyday Life
JANE HINDLEY (2006)

Ethnicity and Everyday Life
CHRISTIAN KARNER (2007)

Risk, Vulnerability and Everyday Life
IAIN WILKINSON (2007)

Cities and Everyday Life
DAVID PARKER (2007)

ETHNICITY AND EVERYDAY LIFE

CHRISTIAN KARNER

Routledge
Taylor & Francis Group

LONDON AND NEW YORK

First published 2007
by Routledge
2 Park Square, Milton Park, Abingdon, Oxon OX14 4RN

Simultaneously published in the USA and Canada
by Routledge
270 Madison Avenue, New York, NY 10016

*Routledge is an imprint of the Taylor & Francis Group, an informa
Business*

Typeset in Garamond and Scala Sans by
Florence Production Ltd, Stoodleigh, Devon
Printed and bound in Great Britain by
TJ International Ltd, Padstow, Cornwall

British Library Cataloguing in Publication Data
A catalogue record for this book is available from the British
Library

Library of Congress Cataloging in Publication Data
Karner, Christian.
  Ethnicity and everyday life/Christian Karner.
      p. cm.
    Includes bibliographical references and index.
  1. Ethnicity.   2. Ethnic groups.   3. Group identity.   I. Title.
  GN495.6.K373 2007
  305.8–dc22   2006024256

ISBN: 978–0–415–37065–3 (hbk)
ISBN: 978–0–415–37066–0 (pbk)
ISBN: 978–0–203–03047–9 (ebk)

CONTENTS

SERIES EDITOR'S FOREWORD

"The New Sociology" is a Series that takes its cue from massive social transformations currently sweeping the globe. Globalization, new information technologies, the techno-industrialization of warfare and terrorism, the privatization of public resources, the dominance of consumerist values: these developments involve major change to the ways people live their personal and social lives today. Moreover, such developments impact considerably on the tasks of sociology, and the social sciences more generally. Yet, for the most part, the ways in which global institutional transformations are influencing the subject-matter and focus of sociology have been discussed only in the more advanced, specialized literature of the discipline. I was prompted to develop this Series, therefore, in order to introduce students – as well as general readers who are seeking to come to terms with the practical circumstances of their daily lives – to the various ways in which sociology reflects the transformed conditions and axes of our globalizing world.

Perhaps the central claim of the Series is that sociology is fundamentally linked to the practical and moral concerns of everyday life. The authors in this Series – examining topics all the way from the body to globalization, from self-identity to consumption – seek to demonstrate the complex, contradictory ways in which sociology is a necessary and very practical aspect of our personal and public lives. From one angle, this may seem uncontroversial. After all, many classical sociological analysts as well as those associated with the classics of social theory emphasized the practical basis of human knowledge, notably Emile Durkheim, Karl Marx, Max Weber, Sigmund Freud, and George Simmel, among many others. And yet there are major respects in which the professionalization of academic sociology during the latter period of the twentieth century led to a retreat from the everyday issues and moral basis of sociology itself. (For an excellent discussion of the changing relations between practical and professional sociologies see Charles Lemert, *Sociology After the Crisis*, Second Edition, Boulder: Paradigm, 2004). As worrying as such a retreat from the practical and moral grounds of the discipline is, one of the main consequences of recent global transformations in the field of sociology has been a renewed emphasis on the mediation of everyday events and experiences by distant social forces, the intermeshing of the local and global in the production of social practices, and on ethics and moral responsibility at both the individual and collective levels. "The New Sociology" Series traces out these concerns across the terrain of various themes and thematics, situating everyday social practices in the broader context of life in a globalizing world.

In *Ethnicity and Everyday Life*, Christian Karner explains why ethnicity is a growing source of political conflict in our globalizing world, producing and transforming multiplex patterns of inequality and domination. Against this background, Karner says that we should understand ethnicity from a new sociological perspective that highlights three interrelated dimensions: (1) the social structures of ethnicity which simultaneously enable and constrain human agency; (2) the complex, contradictory cognitive mapping of ethnicity which provides a map of ourselves and others in the world; and, (3) the everyday experience of ethnicity, in terms of its emotional reach, biographical context and interpersonal dynamics. This triangular analysis, it seems to me, challenges much orthodox sociological thinking about the conditions and consequences of ethnicity, and one of the great merits of this book – appearing as it does under the imprint of "The New Sociology" – is to broaden the sociological terrain of ethnicity studies into the fields of social anthropology and history. Karner certainly writes an interdisciplinary, insightful and rapid narrative of the ongoing force of ethnicity in these early years of the twenty-first century, and the book undoubtedly supplies a historical, critical and, yes, political positioning to the relation between ethnicity and the everyday which is missing in many mainstream accounts of the topic.

Karner's powers as a sociological analyst are on display in this broad yet critical study of the facts, fantasies, fears and forebodings generated and reproduced through processes of ethnicity – its social ascriptions, categorizations and group identifications. From traveller gypsies to diaspora communities, from ethnic outsiders and minorities to the resurgence of current neo-nationalisms trading in severe social exclusions, Karner has a razor-sharp understanding of the multi-faceted place of ethnicity in the everyday lives of individuals and groups struggling to cope with, and react to, a world of Others. Whether discussing anti-Semitism and the plight of the Jews in Hitler's death camps or horrific ethnic cleansing as witnessed in the Balkans of former Yugoslavia, Karner tracks the interplay of ethnic hatred, ideological indoctrination and the (however minimal) power-to-do-otherwise that comprises instantiations of racial violence with precision and crisp intelligence. And what of the future of ethnicity in a globalizing world? Few would dispute that the vision of a free, open, liberal-democratic society appears increasingly fragile in the wake of defensive ethnicities, closed communities and the resurgence of racial hatreds that have been unlocked as a result of 9/11, religious extremism and the War on Terror. However Karner, wisely, knows that to analyse a social pathology is not to dissolve it. Equally wisely, he knows that the promise of multicultural and cosmopolitan visions of society underscore the promise of ethnicities in which individuals and groups should be able to preserve and enjoy their cultures. It is hard to know where all of this leads in the current phase of globalization; but as Karner identifies, ethnicity – as a value of difference, diversity and of the freedoms of living – is central to any reflective and autonomous notion of what a good society would look like.

ACKNOWLEDGEMENTS

This book is premised on the conviction that there is a pressing need for sociological understanding of 'everyday ethnicity' in the contemporary world. In addition to giving me the opportunity to think my way through topics of acute political relevance, working on this book has been a greatly stimulating and enjoyable experience. It is therefore more than fitting to start by thanking some of the people and institutions whose support has made what follows possible.

First of all, I would like to thank Constance Sutherland, Ann Carter, Gerhard Boomgaarden and Anthony Elliott for their trust and some much-needed editorial help along the way. A fundamental debt of gratitude goes to the Leverhulme Trust, whose support at a slightly earlier stage in my academic life – in the shape of a special research fellowship – facilitated much of the research informing this book. Parts of Chapter 2 have previously appeared in an article entitled 'Theorising power and resistance among "Travellers"' that was published in volume 14, number 3 of *Social Semiotics* (see http://www.tandf.co.uk/journals/titles/10799893.asp); I would like to thank Taylor & Francis for granting permission to reuse the material in question. Moreover, I would like to express my gratitude to the following colleagues in the School of Sociology and Social Policy at the University of Nottingham, who have provided intellectual stimulation as well as some much-appreciated everyday acts of friendship: Alan and Meryl Aldridge, Esther Bott, Julia O'Connell Davidson, David Parker, Nick Stevenson and Amal Treacher. Finally (and as always), I would like to thank my family and Chrysanthi for their unconditional patience, understanding and support.

INTRODUCTION

In the earliest stages of working on this book, I once scribbled the following comments on a paper napkin:

> It is the shortest day of the year. I am in a restaurant in Munich, having food widely recognized as Italian. The waiter is a very kind young man of Turkish ancestry whom certain widespread, highly simplistic, misleading and often dangerous stereotypes might construct as 'outwardly gay'; he easily switches from Turkish, when speaking to a group of obviously regular customers, to Bavarian German. The music is of the popular, anglophone variety one hears in restaurants all around the world (though perhaps 'interrupted' by musical traces of whichever ethnicity is represented in any given setting). Here I am, an Austrian resident of the UK, working on a book on *Ethnicity and Everyday Life*, having Italian food in Munich, speaking to the Turkish-German waiter in 'my' dialect of German that is still intelligible in the southern parts of Germany: is ethnicity all around and in me? Or would saying this miss other, equally (or perhaps more) important 'stories' — stories about citizenship and class, about consumerism and postmodern identities, about highly unhelpful stereotypes of gender and sexuality, stories about perhaps one of the last truly wintry nights in times of global warming?

There is much in these comments that is pertinent to this book. First, they encapsulate a scene partly to do with ethnicity and everyday life, as well as their intersection. As such, these comments capture much that is of relevance to the pages and analyses that follow. Second, some of these comments echo Steve Fenton's observations that in looking for ethnicity we can be reasonably sure to find 'it', that ethnicity is not a 'unitary phenomenon' reducible to a single theory, and that sociological analysis should aim to illuminate the various structural and historical circumstances under which ethnicity comes to matter (Fenton 2003: 134–159, 179–180); that ethnicity matters at the beginning of the twenty-first century is indisputable; what shall preoccupy us here is the attempt to understand how and why ethnic traditions, cultural practices and ideas of group belonging have acquired renewed appeal and mobilizing power at this particular point in history. Third, my comments echo existing studies (e.g. Song 2003) of ethnic identities as negotiated, albeit under conditions of profoundly unequally distributed power, by people with agency and several sources of possible identification at their disposal. Identity is fast becoming an 'over-used' but ill-defined concept; rather than offering an explanation, it requires explaining (e.g. Malešević 2002), not least since constant 'identity talk' is juxtaposed to many people's everyday lives that are shaped by several 'cultures' (to introduce another ubiquitous and equally ill-defined term): none of us *is* just one thing, *belongs* to just one group and *has* just one identity; and yet we are constantly surrounded by a language that emphasizes being, belonging and having. Among the aims of this book is the attempt to sociologically think through these prominent discourses, to question them, and to discuss them in relation to the multiple, 'intersecting' axes of power and inequality (Brah 1996) within which our lives are embedded.

My 'napkin diary' also raises a number of issues related to everyday life. As we shall see, both ethnicity and the everyday are complex concepts that belie straightforward definition; in the academic realms of the social sciences and the humanities, they are much-debated and frequently contested concepts, both of which involve discussions of power and its effects. Projecting some of these debates on to my earlier quoted reflections, we may ask questions about the political significance of being served Italian pizza by a Turkish-German waiter in Munich on a December evening, 'accompanied' by (almost) universally distributed and recognized popular music, and to the wider backdrop of a global tourist industry and climate change. On one level, this may be read as a scene of enjoyment, pleasure and some inter-cultural communication. On another level, we may remember the feminist slogan that 'the personal is political' and turn it into an assertion of the seemingly trivial being political insofar as it helps sustain or challenge existing structures of power and inequality: the appropriation of, or possible resistance to, common stereotypes thus becomes a political act, as does a trip to Munich (I had, a few hours earlier, been a customer of low-cost air travel), as does the consumption of food and music. Quoting from a book on *Cultural Citizenship*, '[w]hether sorting the rubbish, watching television or changing a nappy, we are never outside of political concerns' (Stevenson 2003: xiii).

A final introductory comment on my 'diary entry' should be made: it positions parts of my own biography in relation to others'. Studying social life involves both other people and our own lives; studying ethnicity requires an appreciation that 'it' affects not only often disempowered minorities but also relatively powerful 'ethnic majorities' (Fenton 2003). In conversation with the writer and civil rights activist James Baldwin, the American anthropologist Margaret Mead (Baldwin and Mead 1971: 105) once remarked how important it was for her students to become conscious of their own ethnicities before embarking on long-term fieldwork in geographically and culturally distant parts of the globe. Following on from this, studying ethnicity in everyday life involves and requires a dialogue with, and understanding of, ourselves (or at least of the parts we can access and understand) as well as others. This book hopes to draw readers into such dialogue aimed at understanding how ethnicity matters, though in vastly different forms, contexts and to different degrees (as well as, crucially, in relation to other social forces and phenomena), in all our biographies and everyday lives at the beginning of the twenty-first century.

ABOUT THIS BOOK

The common identification of ethnicity with culture and descent raises more questions than it can answer. This book explores some of those issues and focuses in particular on the significance of ethnicity in people's everyday lives as well as on the relationship between culture – itself now widely acknowledged as a contested and hard-to-define concept – and ethnicity. Following an introductory discussion of the concepts of 'ethnicity' and 'the everyday' respectively, I present several empirical case studies to examine a series of questions that include the following: How are ethnic groups constructed, shaped and encroached upon by external power structures? How do ethnic communities in turn resist? How are power and human agency being exercised within ethnic groups? Can ethnicity and everyday life be related to debates about nationalism and national identities? What are the effects of migration, living in 'diaspora communities', economic crisis and/or political marginalization on people's sense of (cultural) self? How might the concept of 'identity' and its relation to cultural ideas, practices and institutions be best understood? Might the era since the end of the Cold War be described as an age of ethnicity? If so, what can theories of globalization and/or postmodernity add to the sociological study of ethnicity?

Chapter 1 discusses the key concepts addressed in this book – ethnicity and the everyday respectively. Drawing on seminal literature, I propose analytical frameworks for both ethnicity and everyday life which inform the empirical case studies presented in the remainder of the book. My framework for understanding ethnicity revolves around the following three interrelated key dimensions: first, ethnicity as a set of structures that simultaneously constrain and enable social action; second, ethnicity as a cognitive way of interpreting, or making sense of, the world; and third, ethnicity as a biographically grounded, emotionally charged way of living, experiencing, perceiving and remembering (everyday) life situations. My framework for understanding the everyday foregrounds the following three parameters: power, history/historicity, and consciousness/reflexivity (or lack thereof). The subject matter outlined in Chapter 1 straddles the disciplinary boundaries between sociology, social anthropology and history. The chapter therefore concludes by briefly addressing the relevance and contribution these and related academic disciplines are capable of making to an understanding of ethnicity and everyday life. I argue for dialogue and conceptual borrowing between these disciplines, while underlining sociology's distinctive contribution to the study of ethnicity and everyday life.

Chapter 2 applies Richard Jenkins' theoretical work on *Rethinking Ethnicity* (1997) to Traveller 'Gypsies'. Following a brief historical/empirical overview of various groups commonly designated as 'Roma', 'Travellers' or 'Gypsies', I delineate Traveller communities in the UK as my main case study, although recent research on Roma communities in Central and Eastern Europe will also be discussed. Jenkins' distinction between 'social categorization' and 'group identification' as two separate yet dialectically interrelated processes constitutive of ethnicity frames the analysis presented in this chapter. Social classification refers to the external imposition of a classificatory grid on populations and thus involves powerful outsiders in the construction and reproduction of group boundaries and cultural communities. Group identification, on the other hand, describes people's experience of solidarity and meaning as self-identifying group members. Using a range of existing literature, I demonstrate that Traveller communities have been the object of social classification and external control in various historical and geographical contexts. I pay particular attention to some of the 'disciplinary mechanisms' (Foucault 1991 [1975]) characteristic of modern attempts to exclude and/or assimilate a group widely constructed as both culturally alien and threatening. This is followed by an analysis of Traveller resistance against sedentary power. Drawing on Judith Okely's ethnographic work (1983), I discuss everyday activities such as cooking, washing, Travellers' organization of space and time and gendered division of labour as – in Michel De Certeau's terminology (1984) – 'tactics' of resistance employed in certain marginalized communities. Finally, I discuss the exercise of (and resistance to) patriarchal and inter-generational power *within* Traveller communities.

Chapter 3 examines the everyday experience and articulation of ethnic identities in the context of diaspora communities variously identified as British South Asian, as Pakistani, Indian or Bangladeshi, as Muslim, Hindu or Sikh, as Punjabi, Gujarati or of other regional origins. Following a brief overview of diverse histories of migration within the 'South Asian diaspora', I examine similarly heterogeneous experiences of family life and cultural reproduction, economic hardship or success, political marginalization or self-assertion. Particular emphasis will be put on everyday lives that are often, and contrary to popular stereotypes, best described by the terminology of hybridity and syncretism: rather than being determined by one particular '(Asian) tradition', many people's everyday lives are negotiated at the 'intersections' and in the overlaps of diverse cultural influences. Moreover, experiences of ambivalence and translation affect everyone inhabiting what Avtar Brah (1996) calls a 'diaspora space' that is structured by several 'axes of differentiation' and inequality (e.g. ethnicity, nationality, class, gender). At the heart of this chapter lies Stuart Hall's seminal definition of identities not as essences or *roots* but as 'ongoing projects of becoming' or *routes* (1996: 4). Rather than the static and one-dimensional phenomena they are widely believed to be, identities are shown to be subject to ongoing negotiations. These are shaped by experiences and memories of migration and settlement, by racial marginalization, exclusion and discrimination, as well as by group-internal struggles over self-definitions, role compliance and cultural change. In addition to being constrained by multiple structures of power, identities involve individuals' agency and must be understood in historical context. This is demonstrated with reference to everyday lives and cultural practices that frequently belie official categories and labels, as shown by some excellent studies of the multi-ethnic London suburb of Southall (Gillespie 1995; Baumann 1996) and by relevant forms of cultural production by and for second- and third-generation 'British Asians'.

In Chapter 4 I explore identity politics and the everyday among an 'ethnic majority' (Fenton 2003; Kaufmann 2004) – both the explicitly articulated discourses of belonging and the often taken-for-granted cultural practices of a politically and demographically dominant group. As such, this discussion relates to the resurgence of ethno-national movements and ideologies observed across large parts of the contemporary world as arguably one of its defining characteristics. The empirical case study underpinning Chapter 4 will be of contemporary Austria. Drawing on Zygmunt Bauman's (1993) rediscovery of the concept of 'the stranger' first discussed by Georg Simmel, I examine illustrative and *competing* discourses that provide different definitions of the relationship between the Austrian 'national self' and 'ethnic minorities'/'outsiders', and therefore play a part in the ongoing (re-)production and contestation of group boundaries and identities. This involves an analysis of everyday cultural practices that, albeit sometimes inadvertently, cross-cut and subvert ethnic–national boundaries. I also draw attention to forms of cultural production becoming a political medium for challenging and resisting nationalist exclusion employed by members of the dominant group (e.g. Karner 2002). Echoing Stuart Hall's already mentioned re-conceptualization of 'identities' as unstable and incomplete processes of becoming, I thus examine the contrast between certain political discourses that draw rigid boundaries and everyday cultural/signifying practices that challenge such boundaries by celebrating cultural hybridity/syncretism.

Returning to the argument that the sociology of ethnicity and the everyday must strive for historical contextualization, Chapter 5 explores the significance and appeal of ethnic identities to the backdrop of contemporary globalizing processes. This discussion therefore echoes and develops recent reminders that ethnicity matters, and can only be understood, in the context of particular structural circumstances (e.g. Fenton 2003; Malešević 2004). There are strong indications that ethnic identities have acquired renewed salience and mobilizing potential in the post-Cold-War world: from the above-mentioned nationalist resurgences to an infamous list of ethnic atrocities and conflicts since 1989; arguably, on the level of the everyday, previously taken-for-granted cultural 'backdrops' to people's lives are becoming the reflexive basis of self-definition and politics; languages, national/ethnic/regional identities and histories are being discussed, reflected on, written and read about; implicit in all of this are clear delineations of 'us' from 'them'. This chapter relates these phenomena to the sociology of contemporary global-ization: as 'resistance identities' protesting against real or feared exclusion from the global *network society* (Castells 1996, 1997); as 'neo-tribal movements' indicative of a 'yearning for community' in an individualized society of consumerism and growing economic inequalities (Bauman 1992, 1998, 2001); as a symptom of life in the 'risk society' (Beck 1992); as a reaction to a world dominated by multinational companies and the insecurities generated by the dismantling of yesteryear's welfare systems (Beck 2000). The case study used to explore these issues (and following a brief discussion of the post-war history of migration to northern and western Europe) will be of contemporary forced migration and everyday exclusions experienced by asylum seekers, the significance of ethnic ties in their day-to-day lives, as well as their vilification in much media and popular discourse.

The conclusion summarizes the arguments presented in the book and notes the 'dual character' of ethnicity: on the one hand, a political tool of exclusion and, on the other, a – in some contexts much-needed – source of meaning, solidarity and identity. The conclusion also emphasizes human agency as a key dimension and recurring theme by briefly referring to Martin Gilbert's study of *The Righteous* (2002): these were some 19,000 'ordinary' European citizens who, during World War II, risked their own lives to save Jews from deportation to Hitler's death camps. Relevant to many of the themes explored here (e.g. power and resistance, cultural exclusion, identity, persecution, human agency and historical context), the Righteous epitomized ideological resistance and moral responsibility in a context where racial hatred, ideological indoctrination, intimidation and fear, ethnic violence and genocide had become part of everyday life.

HOW ETHNICITY MATTERS

The attentive reader may have picked up on a central, though so far merely asserted statement made at the beginning of this introductory chapter: that ethnicity matters in our current era is, I stated, indisputable. This statement requires further illustration, not least as it provides part of the rationale underpinning this book and, I presume, part of the assumptions likely to be motivating its readers. The most problematic word in this statement is the verb 'to matter'; it hides much more than it reveals, begging the question as to what 'mattering' entails. Put simply, we may distinguish between two forms of 'mattering'. First, things matter if they make other things happen, thus acting as a cause in a chain of events. It is in this sense that ethnicity is widely assumed to 'matter'. As we shall explore in due course, ethnicity intersects in important ways with cultural and religious phenomena. At the same time, the concepts of culture, ethnicity and religion remain undefined in much popular usage while being misused as catch-all explanations for things as varied as social exclusion and economic success, terrorism, genocide, street crime and binge-drinking. Some simplistic popular discourses never tire of suggesting that these and innumerable other social phenomena (and, more often than not, social ills) are caused by 'cultures', religious beliefs or ethnic divisions. Along with most contributions to the academic study of ethnicity, this book challenges such pseudo-explanations that mis-portray a concept they do not take the trouble to discuss let alone define as the alleged cause of far more complex phenomena and problems. Such accounts are not only intellectually lazy and ultimately untenable, they are also rarely politically innocent.

This has been compellingly demonstrated by the American political scientist Paul Brass. In a book entitled *Theft of an Idol* (1997), Brass examines several local incidents of violence – including the theft of a religious idol, a mass brawl and the rape of a girl – in the setting of his fieldwork in northern India. Influenced by the French theorist Michel Foucault, Brass examines the common (local and national) assumption that these incidents were 'ethnic' in nature, that they reflected a long-standing, primordial clash of fundamentally different and mutually antagonistic cultural and religious groups. However, Brass goes on to challenge these popular accounts by analysing how such localized incidents of violence are represented and portrayed in the media, by local, regional and national politicians and other social actors. His conclusion is striking: he demonstrates that the origins of the incidents were often ambiguous, hard to define and not at all clearly ethnic in character. However, the media, politicians and others then applied certain pre-existing discourses in their interpretations and explanations of violence:

> [T]he publicized version of many so-called . . . communal riots in India . . . are constructions upon events . . . open to a multiplicity of interpretations. . . . It is often the case that the precipitating incidents arise out of situations that are either not inherently ethnic/communal in nature or are ambiguous in character, that their transformation into . . . communal incidents depends upon the attitudes . . . taken by local politicians and local representatives of state authority, and that their ultimate elevation into grand communal confrontations depends upon

> their further reinterpretation by the press and extralocal . . . authorities.
> The 'official' interpretation that finally becomes universally accepted is
> often . . . very far removed, often unrecognizable, from the original
> events. This is particularly the case with . . . riots that are labelled
> 'communal' or 'Hindu–Muslim' riots.
>
> (Brass 1997: 6)

It is therefore the interpretations that are circulated after the event
that portray ethnicity as an independent variable and hence *construct*
the incidents in question as allegedly caused by deep-seated ethnic/
religious identities. In other words, a violent incident takes place
and people subsequently offer interpretations of what happened. Such
interpretations draw on already existing discourses, the most
dominant or widely used of which emphasize the significance of
ethnicity. Ethnicity, in other words, may come to the fore in the *post-
hoc* explanations used by people rather than in the precipitating
incidents. Moreover, social actors (including the media and
politicians) draw on interpretations emphasizing ethnicity in a self-
interested manner, because it suits their agendas. Politicians thus
appeal to a Hindu majority electorate by constructing incidents of
violence as 'ethnic in nature': such accounts polarize the population
into two groups, one of which is told that it ought to fear the other
and that the politicians offering the interpretations in question are
the ones to be voted for, since they will offer protection for an
allegedly threatened 'in-group'. Put another way, while the reasons
underlying a violent incident may be hard to discern, people demand
explanations and certain (privileged) social actors – most notably the
media and politicians – are in a position to offer and impose them.
While serving certain purposes for the social actors enunciating
them, the proposed interpretations are often informed by pre-
existing discourses that misconstruct religion and ethnicity as the
only sources of social identity and as alleged determinants of people's
character, predisposition and behaviour.

Thus we arrive at the second meaning of the verb 'to matter':
taking on board Brass' insights, we may argue that the contemporary
power of ethnicity resides less in its inevitable social effects than in
its imputed effects, that 'it' is much less a singular force determining
people's behaviour than a much-used framework of interpretation

and political mobilization. The power of ethnicity is ascribed to it by social actors, who interpret the world around them through a pervasive prism that *constructs* ethnicity as a powerful force. While the effects of such discursive processes are just as real, there is (at least) one crucial difference between the simplistic accounts Brass challenges and the constructivist alternative he offers: the former take human agency out of the picture, reducing social action and complex conflicts to an assumed and ill-defined entity variously referred to as a cultural, religious or ethnic identity; constructivist approaches, on the other hand, do not deny the 'real-ness' of ethnicity but locate it in the realm of *human understanding, interpretation and meaning*. As a result, complex social processes and realities are reopened to critical investigation and our shared involvement in continually (re-)making our social world is acknowledged (see below). Such analytical 'advantages' notwithstanding, we are also justified in questioning if this constructivist alternative captures ethnicity in its full 'ontological' complexity (e.g. Fenton 2003: 2–4) – in its social contexts, historical embeddedness, everyday manifestations and existential significance to (many) social actors. We will discuss these issues in Chapter 1.

For now, the main remaining question is if ethnicity really does indisputably 'matter' in this second sense of the word, as a way of experiencing, making sense of and – in the process – constructing the world. In other words, does our everyday life provide evidence that people and institutions use and/or impose the prism of ethnic, national, religious, and racial identities in the things they say, the way they interpret and act in the world? To most people involved in the study of ethnicity the answer to this question would be a resounding 'yes'. However, we must of course do better than resort to a mere assertion of disciplinary conviction. By way of providing an illustration and some (though admittedly somewhat anecdotal) evidence supporting such a 'yes', let me partly borrow an approach pioneered in Michael Billig's study of *Banal Nationalism* (1995): to demonstrate the taken-for-granted delineation of 'the nation' from 'outsiders' in everyday language, Billig conducts a one-day survey of ten British daily newspapers published on 28 June 1993. He shows that – in spite of their different political preferences, journalistic registers and intended audiences – all papers address, and in the process help reproduce, a similar national 'us'. The existence of national identities is assumed as a given, '*the* nation becomes *the* place, as the centre of the universe contracts to the national borders' (Billig 1995: 115); or, in the terminology of the French cultural theorist Roland Barthes, a creation of culture and history (i.e. national borders and groups) is 'naturalized', mis-portrayed as a seemingly predetermined and inevitable fact of nature. Without here emulating such a systematic analysis, it seems instructive to conclude this Introduction by describing the contents of (merely) one British national daily newspaper, on the randomly chosen day that was 10 December 2004. The paper in question was the left-of-centre broadsheet the *Guardian*, which unlike some of its tabloid counterparts is not known for reducing complex realities to simple formulae or for demonizing ethnic 'otherness'. The pervasiveness of news related to ethnicity on a randomly chosen (and arguably relatively ordinary) day would appear to provide some corroborating evidence for the claim that ethnicity features prominently in the way many people understand, interpret and act in the world at this particular point in history: The *Guardian*'s lead article on 10 December 2004 reported on the catastrophic effects of the AIDS pandemic on sub-Saharan Africa; this was followed by articles on a tragically prophetic assessment that London was under continuing threat from *al-Qaida*-style terrorist attacks, on Europe's various far Right parties contemplating a cross-border coalition, and on a previous (now condemned) operation intended to prevent Czech Roma from claiming asylum in the UK; coverage of French plans to 'nationalize' Islam by calling on *imams* to take university courses (on language, history, culture and civil law), of a football club expressing anger at being charged with racism, and of a national cricket board concerned with a potential 'flood' of foreign players, completing the picture of questions of ethnicity, nationality and 'race' underpinning many national, international and sports-related news.

None of these issues can of course be reduced to ethnicity, nor did any of the related coverage imply that they could. However, what such 'everyday news' suggests is that ethnicity is indeed ubiquitous in the world as many of us know, experience and make sense of it at the beginning of the twenty-first century. As emphasized earlier, this is not at all to attribute (singular) causal power to our own or other people's ethnicity. A key aim pursued in what follows is to throw some light on the considerably more complex and multifaceted place and significance of ethnicity in the everyday lives of individuals and groups as they negotiate the contradictions, dilemmas, inequalities, anxieties and (at least occasional) joys of our global age.

1

ETHNICITY AND EVERYDAY LIFE

I hope readers will forgive me for starting another chapter with a biographical snippet: my first self-conscious engagement with the concept of ethnicity occurred in the early 1990s to the backdrop of the collapse of former Yugoslavia, as the world watched in horror the unfolding of ethnic cleansing in the Balkans. The demise of communism, so a then widely circulating explanatory narrative went, had allowed suppressed but deep-seated identities and divisions to resurface; ethnic conflict and violence were, so such simplistic accounts continued, the inevitable result. While the over-simplifications inherent in these self-proclaimed 'explanations' have been revealed and challenged since (e.g. Gilliland 1995), they none the less contain a set of assumptions that provide a suitable point of departure and subsequent criticism for this chapter. First, these accounts assumed ethnicity to be an innate, deeply engrained determinant of people's behaviour and loyalties that overrode both individual agency and alternative sources of identity. Second, these accounts reproduced the common association of ethnicity with conflict (Hutchinson and Smith 1996: 3). Third, they also contained some assumptions about everyday life, portraying ethnicity as a force disruptive and ultimately destructive of the previously largely harmonious lives shared by neighbours and citizens of a state that was no more; arguably, the accounts in question hence also implied that peaceful everyday routines were incompatible with ethnic identities assumed to be inevitably divisive. In what follows, I cast a critical eye on each of these assumptions: I discuss the much-debated relationship between ethnic groups and traditions on the one hand, and individuals' lives, ideas and behaviours on the other; moreover, I question the very problematic conflation of ethnicity with conflict as well as the equally problematic association of the everyday with the supposedly trivial, apolitical and culturally insignificant. In other words, this chapter sets itself the task of working through complex bodies of literature on the two concepts at the heart of this book: ethnicity and everyday life. Rather than establishing easy-to-digest working definitions, I provide multi-dimensional conceptual frameworks for thinking about ethnicity and everyday life, which will guide the analysis of my empirical case studies in subsequent chapters. The theoretical groundwork presented here is rounded off by a brief mention of relevant methodological and 'disciplinary' questions: how might we study ethnicity and/in everyday lives, and which academic traditions and disciplinary approaches may guide us along the way?

ETHNICITY

Ideas about racial, national and ethnic groups 'bear strong family resemblances' (Fenton 2003: 8). Nations tend to be associated with territories, state institutions and cultural histories as is reflected in a seminal definition of nationalism as the attempt to 'make culture and polity congruent' (Gellner 1983). While 'race' is primarily associated with physical characteristics, it is now widely acknowledged that 'races' are social constructs rather than biological givens; the choices of physical markers *assumed* to be racial characteristics are historically and culturally variable. As shown by some of the most infamous historical chapters (e.g. slavery, the Holocaust, apartheid), racial classifications have been politically highly significant and tragically consequential as ideological tools variously used to condone inequality, injustice, exploitation, oppression, dehumanization and genocide. Their often terrible political uses stand in tragic contradiction to the fact that modern genetics confirms the biological non-existence of distinct 'racial groupings':

There are two . . . reasons for this. First, there has always been so much interbreeding between human populations that it [is] meaningless to speak of fixed boundaries between races. Second, the distribution of hereditary physical traits does not follow clear boundaries. In other words, there is often greater variation within a 'racial' group than there is systematic variation between two groups.

(Eriksen 1993: 4)

Ethnicity, the third of the three related concepts, is widely associated with culture, descent, group memories/histories and language. So what are the family resemblances that Fenton mentions and that my earlier 'day survey' of the *Guardian* presupposed in emphasizing the prevalence of questions of ethnicity, nationality and 'race'? Apart from the fact that politicians, the media and 'ordinary' social actors frequently use the three concepts interchangeably, a closer look confirms that they share several characteristics. Crucially, and contrary to widespread beliefs that national, ethnic and 'racial' groups are 'naturally occurring' entities, they reflect and rely upon social processes and discourses that *construct* and subsequently *naturalize/ reify* group differences. As such, Benedict Anderson's definition (1983) of the nation as a community 'imagined' against the backdrop of a particular historical and technological context (i.e. the era of capitalism and the printing press) may be partly extended to groups assumed to be 'racial' or ethnic in character (see Jenkins 2002: 21): the facts that racial taxonomies are culturally and historically variable and ethnic boundaries are often contested (see later chapters) show that 'racial' and ethnic categories are context-dependent social constructs – albeit tremendously powerful ones. George Orwell once commented that 'all claims to be better than somebody else because you have a different-shaped skull or speak a different dialect are [of course] entirely spurious, but they are important as long as people believe in them' (1962: 100). Among social scientists, this is known as W.I. Thomas' 'first law of social constructivism: if someone believes a thing, it will affect what he or she does, and it will therefore be real in its consequences' (Jenkins 2002: 21).

A central family characteristic common to ideas about nations, ethnicities and 'races' is thus their propensity to draw boundaries and hence to attribute group membership. These are profoundly political practices that variously reproduce or challenge existing power structures by perpetuating or opposing existing distributions and inequalities of status, wealth and the ability to implement decisions: it is in this sense that a recurring definition of ethnicity as 'politicized culture' (e.g. McCrone 1998; Malešević 2004), the strategic use of cultural characteristics, may be understood. Moreover, most discourses – by which I refer to written and spoken language employed in particular historical contexts, for political purposes and/or with discernible social effects (e.g. Fairclough 1992; Weiss and Wodak 2003) – about national, 'racial' and ethnic groups claim to evoke and articulate a particular type of 'comradeship' (e.g. Spillman 1997): a group solidarity that purports to cross-cut and supersede internal differences of class, status, wealth and power, and hence to 'unify' a group of people in spite of such differences. Later parts of this book will emphasize that such discourses not only overlook persisting power differentials within the groups they construct, but they also ignore human agency, intra-group conflicts and contestation as well as cultural change as near-omnipresent social realities.

Having acknowledged such family characteristics common to various types of perceived and/or self-identifying social collectives, the question remains as to what distinguishes an ethnic community from national and 'racial' groups as its conceptual siblings. A tentative answer to this question is provided by the concept of *ethnie*, defined as 'a named human population with myths of common ancestry, shared historical memories, one or more elements of common culture [e.g. religion, customs, language], a [frequent] link with a homeland and a sense of solidarity among at least some of its members' (Hutchinson and Smith 1996: 6). As far as working definitions go, this is very helpful and captures much that the concept of ethnicity implies to members of ethnic communities and to academics who study them; Hutchinson and Smith draw attention to the existence of a name or label used variously by outsiders and/or members of a given ethnic community themselves; they further underline the significance of a (perceived) past and of a group-specific culture – by which we here refer to more or less widely shared ideas, social practices, norms and forms of social organization; moreover, Hutchinson and Smith observe that ethnic groups are positioned in space as much as in time, as is reflected in frequent emotional attachments to a particular territory, either currently inhabited or considered to be a now lost ancestral homeland; finally, this working definition makes reference to the significance of ethnic co-members recognizing themselves and others as belonging (or not) to the same community, a recognition that implies not only a degree of reflexivity but also often – though by no means invariably – a heightened sense of solidarity with others considered to be part of the 'in-group'. All this being said, a working definition usually constitutes a mere starting point to a debate rather than its finishing line. In this particular case, Hutchinson and Smith's working definition raises numerous important questions, some of which – including the following – will recur throughout this book: *How, and by whom, are 'names' given to groups of people and would these groups, in the absence of such labelling processes, constitute ethnic communities? How might the relationship between cultural ideas and practices on the one hand, and individuals' beliefs and behaviour on the other, be best conceptualized? What, in other words, is the scope for human agency in relation to an ethnic group one is assumed to 'belong to'? Conversely, how do ethnic traditions impact on the lives of social actors? Do ethnic categories and traditions come to matter under particular social circumstances? If so, what are they? Is consciousness of belonging a prerequisite for a cultural community to become an ethnic one?*

Groups and traditions, individuals and circumstances

Among these complex issues, questions pertaining to the relationship between cultures and individuals have preoccupied academics studying ethnicity more than any others. The resulting and long-standing debates have been shaped by competing schools of thought that emphasize the assumed determining force of (ascribed) ethnic identities and the significance of circumstances as well as human agency respectively. The former paradigm, often referred to as *primordialism*, may be thought of as a form of cultural determinism that postulates the more or less non-negotiable power of ethnic ties and is widely associated with a much-quoted passage from Clifford Geertz's *The Interpretation of Cultures*:

> [A] primordial attachment . . . stems from the . . . assumed givens of social existence: immediate contiguity and kin connections . . . [and] the

> given-ness . . . [of] being born into a particular religious community,
> speaking a particular language . . . and following particular practices.
> These congruities of blood, speech, custom . . . are seen to have an
> ineffable, and at times overpowering coerciveness. . . . One is bound to
> one's kinsman . . . one's fellow believer . . . as the result not merely of
> personal affection, practical necessity, common interest, or incurred
> obligation, but at least in great part by virtue of some . . . absolute import
> attributed to the very tie itself. The general strength of such primordial
> bonds . . . differ[s] from person to person, from society to society, and
> from time to time.
>
> (Geertz 1973: 259–260)

There has been considerable debate on whether Geertz has been
wrongly accused of portraying culture and descent as irresistible
determinants of people's loyalties and behaviour. For example,
Richard Jenkins (1997: 45) points out that Geertz merely suggests
that certain ties 'are seen to have an . . . overpowering coerciveness'
and that the strength of the bonds in question varies across
individuals, social formations and historical eras. This assumed
blueprint of ethnic primordialism may therefore, according to such
alternative readings (see also Brubaker *et al*. 2004: 49), be perfectly
compatible with the above-mentioned first law of social
constructivism and its emphasis on the very real consequences of
people's beliefs and perceptions. However, such ongoing debates and
arguably necessary corrections must not detract from an important
observation contained in Geertz's account that any serious discussion
of ethnicity needs to engage with: the fact that membership in
cultural and ethnic groups is widely, though certainly not invariably
or inevitably, *experienced* as an ascribed identity, as a place in the world
one is born into, a social position that can trigger a profound sense
of solidarity with fellow group members, and frequently places the
individual in networks of social relationships and perceived
responsibilities that appear to be if not 'natural' at least self-evident.
Implicit in such observations is another insight crucial to any
discussion of ethnicity: the fact that social bonds, solidarity and
identifications inevitably involve some people and exclude others,
that social identities rely on boundaries delineating 'us' from 'them'.
However, while this recognition is echoed by most studies of (ethnic)

identities (e.g. De Vos and Romanucci-Ross 1995: 361; Baumann and Gingrich 2004), it does not entail an inevitable commitment to primordialism, and there has been, as we shall see, a great deal of debate on the 'nature', origins and negotiability of ethnic boundaries.

In light of the above-mentioned critical rereading of Geertz, the metaphor of a continuum of interpretations may be more apt than the idea of competing schools of thought. That being said, the second major paradigm of ethnicity contained in the literature may be described as a broad 'church' made up of different versions of social constructivism. Richard Jenkins observes that social constructivist approaches to ethnicity and cultural differentiation are premised on an 'appreciation that ethnic identity is situationally variable and negotiable . . . [that] "groups" are not distinct things in a positivist sense . . . [but] contingent and immanently changeable . . . emergent product[s] of interaction and of classificatory processes' (1997: 50). Among such social constructivist approaches we may, taking our cue from Steve Fenton, distinguish between *instrumentalist* and *situational/circumstantial* models respectively: instrumentalist conceptualizations (e.g. Cohen 1969) regard ethnicity as a social and symbolic resource mobilized in the self-interested pursuit of economic and political goals, as a collective strategy of survival, social mobility or group reproduction through historically grounded, though not continuously utilized, channels of communication and networks of support and solidarity. Not entirely dissimilarly, situational/circumstantial accounts hold that an individual's 'actual identity deployed or made relevant changes according to . . . social situations' and that 'ethnic identity is important in some contexts and not others' (Fenton 2003: 84). Miri Song's observations, contained in her aptly titled book *Choosing Ethnic Identity*, may be regarded as paradigmatic of the situational model:

> Every group's culture is complex, diverse, and constitutive of a wide variety of practices and . . . traditions, which may espouse different values and positions. No group's culture is static or unidimensional; rather, it is always contested and in flux. . . . [W]e need to see [individuals] as agents who actively negotiate their . . . ethnic identities in relation to both insiders and outsiders in a multitude of contexts. Within limits, minority individuals can contest the meaning of a particular ethnic identity,

> including the terms of . . . group membership. For instance, what does it mean to be Chinese in Britain today? Does it mean speaking a Chinese dialect and partnering with a Chinese person? Or does it mean being informed by both Chinese and British identities and cultures?
>
> (Song 2003: 42–43)

Social constructivist approaches to ethnicity may be traced to the early work by the Norwegian social anthropologist Fredrik Barth who famously defined ethnicity as a form of social organization based on the drawing and reproduction of group boundaries. Ethnic groups, Barth observed, were 'categories of ascription [by others] and identification by the actors themselves' (1969: 10). He thus drew attention to the important and subsequently much-discussed fact that the construction of boundaries and hence of communities implicates often powerful outsiders as well as group members. Crucially, such boundary drawing, ascription of membership and identification with a particular community are ongoing social processes and accomplishments rather than the inevitable result of a 'natural', pre-existing state of affairs. Moreover, and in contrast to the common association of ethnicity with the notion of a shared culture, Barth emphasized that the continuity of an ethnic group required merely the 'maintenance of a boundary', often despite changes to the cultural characteristics and organizational forms associated with it; articulating a paradigmatic shift in the study of ethnicity, Barth stressed that 'the critical focus of investigation . . . becomes the ethnic boundary that defines the group, not the cultural stuff that it encloses' (1969: 15).

Barth's legacy, his focus on the social processes of boundary maintenance and his acknowledgement of historical changes occurring within ethnic communities, resurfaces in parts of the empirical case studies contained in this book. While emphasizing people's everyday lives (and the relations of power and inequality in which they are embedded) and introducing the crucial variable of cultural change, Barth's work also takes note of a further core concern of sociological enquiry – human agency; he thus observes that 'boundaries may persist despite what may figuratively be called the "osmosis" of personnel through them' (1969: 21). The metaphor of osmosis allows for the hugely important fact that not every individual regards him- or herself as equally or permanently 'defined' by the boundaries that encircle them and the social categories to which they are deemed to 'belong'. To illustrate such 'flow of personnel' across persisting ethnic boundaries, we may think of individuals who marry outside their ethnic group, often to their co-ethnics' considerable disapproval, who migrate or who convert to a different religion. As I will argue in later chapters, a convincing account of ethnicity and everyday life must be able to detect and analyse such exercises of human agency.

Recent contributions to the sociological study of ethnicity have asked the important question: Do some social constructivist reactions against the alleged determinism of primordial models run the risk of throwing the baby out with the bathwater? Is there not quite clearly something about ethnicity that many people experience as a profoundly important and often lifelong emotional attachment to what they regard as 'their' culture, history, language and community? If so, how successful are models of ethnicity that rely exclusively on a situational, circumstantial or instrumental conceptualization of such a 'spell'? And, as suggested by Steve Fenton, is it not perhaps the case that primordial and social constructivist accounts raise two rather different analytical questions concerning the 'nature of the ethnic tie' and the contexts in which it becomes important respectively? Fenton thus points out that 'someone may have an ascribed ethnic identity which is embedded in their personality and life experience, yet still perceive the circumstances under which it may be instrumental to deploy it' (2003: 84). Our next challenge thus resides in locating an analytical model capable of reconciling the enduring effects of people's enculturation into a group (without reverting to a crude form of determinism and stereotyping) on the one hand, with contextual variation, human agency and historical change on the other. As we shall see, such a model requires a clarification of both the 'culture concept' and of the relationship between culture and ethnicity.

Culture/*habitus*, crisis/politics

Given the association of ethnicity with cultural characteristics/ boundaries, our understanding of the former will be decisively shaped by our conceptualization of the latter; in other words, much hinges on our approach to the concept of culture, itself one of the most widely used yet often most vaguely defined of notions. In order to advance our discussion, we are well advised to turn to Raymond Williams, a key figure in the history of British cultural studies. Williams begins his arguably most influential contribution to the 'culture debate' with an observation also highly pertinent to any discussion of everyday life: culture, he states, is ordinary. Williams then makes an argument that goes some way towards reconciling cultural histories and group socialization with human agency and cultural change. Culture, he insists, consists of two key aspects: 'the known meanings and directions, which its members are trained to' and 'the new observations and meanings, which are offered and tested'; culture is thus always simultaneously traditional *and* creative, known *and* innovative, consisting of both a 'whole way of life [and its] common meanings' *and* 'the special processes of discovery and creative effort' (Williams 1989 [1958]: 4).

A similar conceptualization emerges from Zygmunt Bauman's work on culture as a form of *praxis*, a never completed activity of ordering the world, of organizing behaviour, of 'mak[ing] predictable and manageable the living space of human beings' (1999 [1973]: 74). Bauman stresses that the structuring work performed by culture is an always still ongoing process beset by a defining, 'sense-giving ambivalence': between 'creativity' and 'normative regulation', between 'inventing' and 'preserving', between 'discontinuity' and 'continuation', between 'novelty' and tradition, between routine and 'pattern-breaking', between norms and their transcendence, between the regular and the unique, between the 'monotony of reproduction' and change, between the predictable and the unexpected (Bauman 1999 [1973]: xiv). Both Williams and Bauman thus locate culture in historical context. They detect a defining tension insofar as shared cultural meanings and historically grounded ways of ordering the world are always subject to change, contestation and possible redefinition; culture, then, becomes a process involving meanings and patterns enshrined in the past, the contingencies of the present, and the future-oriented agency of individuals who negotiate the world as they know and experience it both habitually and creatively. As we shall see in subsequent chapters, such a definition of culture, conscious of historical change and the crucial role played by human agency, is a prerequisite for any meaningful understanding of ethnicity and everyday life. First, however, the workings of culture as a process and its relationship to ethnicity deserve further discussion. For this purpose I turn to the (early) work of the French sociologist Pierre Bourdieu.

In *Outline of a Theory of Practice* (1977), Pierre Bourdieu takes as his object of empirical analysis a range of phenomena – observed among the Kabylia of Algeria – highly pertinent to a discussion of ethnicity and everyday life: collective beliefs, relationships of marriage and kinship, popular sayings, the organization of space, time and life cycles, bodily postures and techniques. On a more general level, Bourdieu confronts core questions in the sociology of culture: first, how to understand the relationship between 'objective' structures (both of a material/economic and a cognitive/psychological kind) on the one hand, and individuals' practices, capacity of reflection and possible alternative actions on the other; and, related to this, how best to conceptualize the role of culture in relation to this seeming dichotomy between external constraints and individual behaviour and agency respectively. Bourdieu's answer is an ingenious one, which arguably overcomes a stalemate as old as the social sciences themselves. Rather than committing himself to either a fully deterministic or an unconvincingly voluntaristic model of the social world, Bourdieu re-conceptualizes the role of culture as a set of 'structuring structures' that enable individuals to negotiate external constraints, group-specific histories and ways of living on the one hand, and the contingencies of everyday life on the other. Culture, we may paraphrase, is rethought as the *habitus*, which Bourdieu defines as comprising 'durable, transposable *dispositions*', categories and tastes, a 'socially constituted system of cognitive and motivating structures', 'the basis of perception and appreciation of all subsequent experience', the 'schemes of thought' that serve as the 'basis for the *intentionless invention* of regulated improvisation' (1977: 72–79; emphasis in original). Membership in a cultural community thus entails the acquisition of pervasive and powerful ways of structuring, experiencing and acting in one's surroundings, the internalization of a largely taken-for-granted view of a 'commonsense world', which informs many of one's practices and strategies for dealing with the unexpected. Contrary to his own intentions, critics have accused Bourdieu of still overemphasizing the effects of material constraints and culturally enshrined matrices of *'perceptions, appreciations, and actions'* (1977: 83) at the expense of human agency and social change. Parts of Bourdieu's *Outline* may indeed warrant such criticism after all, he does trace the origins and force of the *habitus* to a person's 'earliest upbringing', partly ascribes an unconscious power to the *habitus*, and suggests that it 'tend[s] to reproduce' the wider social and material conditions – through the actions it guides – that shaped the *habitus* in the first place (Bourdieu 1977: 78–83). However, such criticism overlooks another much less frequently cited part of Bourdieu's analysis, in which he places the *habitus* (or the closely related concept of *doxa*, the 'universe of the undiscussed') in historical context and observes the effects of 'crises', as a result of which the previously taken for granted becomes the object of debate, reflection and disagreement:

> The critique which brings the undiscussed [i.e. *doxa*] into discussion . . . has as the condition of its possibility objective crisis. . . . It is when the social world loses its character as a natural phenomenon that the question of the . . . conventional character of social facts can be raised. . . . Crisis is a necessary condition for a questioning of doxa. . . . The dominated classes have an interest in . . . exposing the arbitrariness of the taken for granted; the dominant classes have an interest in defending the integrity of doxa.
>
> (Bourdieu 1977: 168–169)

Drawing on recent applications of Bourdieu's model (e.g. Vertovec 2000: 63–64, 158–159; Karner 2005a), I argue in later chapters that this offers an illuminating way of defining ethnicity: as the crisis-induced transformation of a previously 'undiscussed' universe of cultural common sense into a realm of debate, struggle and politicization. In such a conceptualization (see also Anthias 2001: 850) the difference between culture and ethnicity is one of reflexivity: culture *becomes* ethnicity when – in the context of rapid and drastic changes and their far-reaching effects – social actors begin to reflect on what they used to think and do in a largely taken-for-granted way prior to the onset of a crisis. The results include conscious struggles for power and resources (as in the above quotation between the dominant and the dominated classes), the self-conscious delineation and maintenance of ethnic boundaries, but also frequently disagreements and debates within the groups thus constructed and reproduced. Developing Bourdieu's insights and applying them to the sociology of ethnicity, we may suggest the following set of relationships:

> Culture : ethnicity :: commonsense : reflexivity :: *habitus* : discourses/ politics

Large parts of the theoretical apparatus underpinning my later case studies are now in place: we will return to the Bourdieu-ian concept of the *habitus* and the transformation of *doxa* into political discourse in times of crises; we will similarly revisit the issue of ethnic boundaries, their reproduction and possible contestation; questions of historical change and human agency will also recur throughout this book. However, before embarking on a discussion of everyday life as our second key theme, we need to explore another crucial question raised earlier: the issue of *how* culture and ethnicity impact on the lives of individuals. Providing a framework for our subsequent case studies, I now explore three dimensions of ethnicity which are clearly interrelated but – for the sake of analytical clarity – are discussed separately.

Ethnicity as *structures of action*

One key to understanding the impact of ethnicity on the (everyday) lives of individuals may be derived from Anthony Giddens' *theory of structuration*, at the heart of which lies an attempt to reconcile questions of social structure with issues of individual agency and practice: not unlike Bourdieu, Giddens argues that the reproduction of the former relies on the latter. More accurately, Giddens uses the idea of the 'duality of structure' to illuminate 'the modes in which [social] systems, grounded in the knowledgeable activities of situated actors who draw upon rules and resources in . . . action contexts, are produced and reproduced in interaction' (1984: 25); cultural norms inform individuals' practices, which in turn – more often than not –

help reproduce existing social relationships. While cultural 'rules and resources' pre-date their use by any one individual, they cannot guard against their own reinterpretation, nor against the formulation of new ideas and hence possible social change. Unlike many of his fellow sociologists, Giddens draws on psychological and psycho-analytical insights to address the important question as to what motivates most individuals most of the time to reproduce existing social relationships through the use of established rules and the participation in routine behaviour. The answer, Giddens suggests (1984, 1991), lies in the individual's need for 'basic trust' in a predictable and hence manageable social environment; ordinary, daily routines play a crucial role in this as 'anxiety-controlling mechanisms' that provide individuals with a sense of 'ontological security' (1984: 50) and are simultaneously instrumental to the reproduction of social relations. At the same time, Giddens stresses that social actors are capable of reflection and that a reflexive engagement with both the self and others is particularly char-acteristic of our contemporary 'late modern' period (1991). According to Giddens' socio-psychological model, much cultural knowledge is tacit, he terms this 'practical consciousness', and is a prerequisite for individuals' social competence and ability to '"go on" in the contexts of social life'; Giddens distinguishes this from 'discursive consciousness', which includes everything 'actors are able to give verbal expression to' (1984: xxiii, 374).

Paraphrasing Giddens, then, much social activity helps reproduce existing social structures. It can only do so through the routine practices of social actors motivated by a deep-seated interest in maintaining a predictable, anxiety-controlling social world. Such practices therefore involve individuals who tacitly know what they are doing and how to do it. At the same time, the (discursive) reflexivity Giddens also emphasizes accounts for the possibility of political challenges, new forms of identity and personal relationships, and hence social change brought about by non-routine, non-conventional, innovative behaviour and ideas. In either case, structure and agency can no longer be treated as alternatives or opposites. Instead, they are closely intertwined, co-dependent and mutually implicated; Giddens expresses this (1984: 25) by stating that 'structure is not "external" to individuals: as memory traces, and as instantiated in social practices, it is in a certain sense more "internal" than exterior. . . . Structure is not to be equated with constraint but is always both constraining and enabling.'

Following Giddens, we may think of ethnicity as simultaneously among the 'rules and resources' (see also Knowles 1999: 119) mobilized by many social actors in sustaining a sense of familiarity (or ontological security) *and* the social structures they reproduce in enacting those rules and resources. Importantly, and as emphasized by Giddens, (ethnic) social structures are thus both constraining and enabling, making certain types of action more likely than others. Yet we shall see that such structured actions, or *structures of action*, also involve knowledgeable and potentially reflexive individuals (endowed with the capacity to act otherwise) and are therefore subject to potential re-negotiation and historical change.

The relevance of ethnicity to many people's (codes of) conduct is easily demonstrated: we merely need to think of rules defining religious observance, permissible and prohibited types of food and drink, the organization of time and space, prescriptions concerning bodily posture and control, ideals about how to live life virtuously, concepts of shame and honour, or strong cultural expectations as to whom one should or should not marry. These and other examples demonstrate the impact of ethnicity on both everyday life and life-cycle events – the special occasions, or rites of passage, marking a person's transition from one social role into another. Such examples corroborate Barth's observation that ethnic identity 'defines the permissible constellations of statuses, or social personalities, which an individual with that identity may assume' (1969: 17). Miri Song similarly observes (2003: 48–49) that 'ethnic and racial identities are often associated with particular "scripts" . . . which stipulate (both implicitly and explicitly) certain forms of behaviour and/or adherence to particular values'. However, while 'ethnic belonging' is undeniably connected to aspects of 'moral control' and provides culturally shared answers to the question as to 'what we must do' (De Vos and Romanucci-Ross 1995: 358), we also need to remember Giddens' insistence that social structures are both constraining and enabling: while it is thus certainly the case, for example, that rules of ethnic endogamy – the strong (and often strongly sanctioned) expectation for people to marry within their group – circumscribe many people's choice of a partner and are instrumental to the reproduction of established social structures, this is by no means inevitably or always experienced as a constraint; adherence to such rules provides many people – though of course not everyone concerned – with a coherent sense of self, cultural belonging and meaning, as well as with a much-needed network of kin, solidarity and support in an often hostile world.

The everyday relevance of ethnicity as *structures of action* emerges with particular clarity from Anita Häusermann Fábos' research among displaced Sudanese families in Cairo. Against the backdrop of the severe political crisis in Sudan, the experience of dislocation and increasing marginalization in Egyptian society, Häusermann Fábos shows that gendered concepts of propriety and modesty play a crucial role as boundary markers among exiled Sudanese. Gender-specific 'codes of behaviour' transmitted in a variety of social institutions (e.g. families, households, mosques) are being re-negotiated in conditions of displacement and socio-economic uncertainty. The latter is exacerbated by widespread unemployment among Sudanese men in Cairo, which has forced their wives into paid work and challenges patriarchal ideas about the division of labour and responsibilities between husbands and wives. Häusermann Fábos shows that in (and arguably because of) such a situation of social dislocation and crisis, gendered codes of modesty, hospitality, chastity and dignity assume ever-greater significance as Sudanese–Egyptian boundary markers:

> Modesty, often thought of in terms of sexual propriety, is not solely a concern for women, despite overt gender symbols like female modesty garments and the social expectation that . . . women . . . maintain social and physical distance from unrelated men. Sudanese men are expected to be discreet about their personal wealth, family connections, and success. Both men and women in Cairo's Sudanese communities consider modest dress an Islamic prescription. . . . By defining Egyptians as 'immodest', Sudanese go beyond modesty as a function of a woman's behaviour to viewing it instead as a fundamental marker of Sudanese identity.
>
> (Häusermann Fábos 2001: 97)

We here encounter a telling example of 'rules and resources' being embodied and enacted by social actors whose culturally sanctioned practices are crucial to the reproduction of existing social relations and structures; in this case, the latter include both the micro-structures of the household and the wider boundaries demarcating Sudanese from Egyptians. In further (inadvertent) corroboration of structuration theory, Häusermann Fábos' informants are reflexive social actors, embedded in their cultural realities yet capable of effecting change; as predicted by Barth (see above), the continuing reproduction of ethnic boundaries is shown to be possible in spite of important cultural changes taking place within the group (i.e. the Sudanese diaspora): Häusermann Fábos reports growing resistance to traditional female circumcision alongside an assertion of Sudanese propriety and hence distinctiveness. Cultures, in other words, change through the agency of individuals, yet ethnic boundaries deemed to be important may persist.

Ethnicity as a *way of seeing*

The second key dimension to ethnicity, and one closely connected to such *structures of action*, is encountered in the ways in which people understand and interpret the world, the way they make life meaningful and predictable, and the positions they allocate to themselves and others in their cognitive 'maps' of the social world. This ties in with a long-standing motif in the study of ethnicity – the observation that human beings seek to provide explanations for the world as they experience and know it; the means by which many ethnic groups do this include myths, religious narratives and beliefs, whose common denominators include 'attempts to explain group origin and continuity' (De Vos and Romanucci-Ross 1995: 357), and hence to account for a community's (mythological) ancestry, historical links to a particular territory and adherence to particular customs and social structures. In an important contribution to this debate, Brubaker *et al.* (2004) argue that this dimension is illuminated by an 'incipient cognitive turn' in the study of ethnicity, which makes use of psychological insights into the workings of the human mind to account for ethnicity as a 'way of seeing the world'. Two cognitive aspects of such ethnic *ways of seeing* deserve particular mention: first, the identity-bestowing differentiation of 'us' from 'them'; and, second, broader frameworks of shared meaning that perform important interpretive work and provide social actors with ready-made theories of the world and their own place in it.

As pointed out above, the construction of 'in-groups' and 'out-groups' through the delineation of boundaries is a defining characteristic of all discourses of collective belonging, whether imposed by powerful outsiders or articulated by self-identifying group members. Identity, whatever else we may mean by the term, involves the distinction of 'us' from 'them'. For our present purposes this is the most significant instance of 'categories structur[ing] and order[ing] the world for us'. As Brubaker *et al.* stress further (2004: 38), categories 'make the natural and social worlds intelligible, interpretable, communicable. . . . Without [them], the world would be a "blooming, buzzing confusion"; experience and action as we know them would be impossible.' In full acknowledgement of the psychological, existential and social significance of classification, recent work on identity construction among various ethnic groups has added a further dimension. It reveals that there are different ways of defining the relationship between categories: 'we' and 'they' may be thought of as mutually exclusive categories, defined in hierarchical terms of relative superiority/inferiority, or may be constructed as related in some situations and radically different in others; moreover, (ethnic) discourses of identity may be shown to negotiate and switch between these various 'grammars of identity' in a context-sensitive fashion (Baumann and Gingrich 2004; Karner 2004a; Postert 2004).

However, Brubaker *et al.* also rightly stress that ethnicity involves more than the classification of social actors by providing ways of 'seeing the social world and interpreting social experience'. To account for such broader theories of the world, they draw on the psychological notion of schemas, defined as 'complex knowledge structures' that are simultaneously representations and 'processors' of information: schemas 'guide perception and recall, interpret experience, generate inferences and expectations, and organize action' (Brubaker *et al.* 2004: 43, 41). Moreover, while most schemas are applied 'automatically, beyond conscious awareness' by many people much of the time, they are 'not forever barred from awareness . . . it is entirely possible to foreground and describe [them]' (Strauss and Quinn 1997: 46). In other words, although some schemas are widely shared and tend to inform a non-reflexive processing of information and interpretation of the world, people are capable of bringing them to the forefront of their consciousness, of critically interrogating and revising them. Agency and historical change are thus compatible with a view of ethnicity as a (schema-guided) 'way of seeing the world'.

Both the centrality of self–other classifications and the cultural significance of broader interpretive theories concerning a group's history and place in the world emerge from Nicholas De Lange's work on Judaism:

> The unity of the Jewish people is [a] powerful idea which has persisted throughout all the vicissitudes of Jewish history. Of course there are real differences of culture and outlook between Jews living in different countries or even within the same country, as indeed there have been since antiquity. But the unity of the whole people is not a pious hope or a goal to be worked for: rather it is a starting point, an axiom which may be taken for granted and from which other ideas and positive actions follow . . . God is addressed as the God of Abraham, Isaac and Jacob, the . . . guardian and redeemer of Israel. The idea of the people of Israel is thus . . . closely bound up with the faith of Israel, which is a faith in the love and power of God, and a faith in the ultimate destiny of all mankind, in which the people of Israel has a special part to play.
>
> (De Lange 1986: 22)

Of course, being Jewish does *not* mean that one inevitably subscribes to this cosmology and view of history. However, it reflects a recurring, more or less widely shared set of ideas, a framework for making sense of the world and Jewish identity, a *way of seeing* the past, the present and the future.

Ethnicity as *structures of feeling*

The third dimension of ethnicity is, while also closely related to the two previous ones, arguably the least tangible. Thinking about culture and ethnicity as *structures of action* and as *ways of seeing* captures much that is important to our discussion; however, it overlooks another highly significant dimension that goes some way towards accounting for the affective salience of ethnicity experienced and/or proclaimed by many people: deeply embedded in our biographies, rooted in our memories and hence often emotionally charged (though such a charge can certainly be a source of pleasure or pain depending on biographical circumstances), is ethnicity not also about the most familiar experiences and practices that clothe people's (early) lives, about sounds, sights and smells that surround us, become familiar, and will trigger memories whenever encountered again? Is ethnicity not also about the taste of familiar foods, the experienced rhythm of daily life, the multiple layers of meaning we detect and negotiate in our first language? Is ethnicity not also – on the level of such experiences, sensations and memories – simultaneously shared and profoundly personal? And if so, how might we think about this dimension sociologically?

Avtar Brah makes a similar point in stating that culture is not only about the customs, values, norms and traditions of the 'social group(s) to which we feel we belong' but also about a *whole spectrum of experiences, modes of thinking, feeling and behaving*'; revealingly, she invites us to contemplate the rather different images and memories culture thus understood is likely to evoke in individuals who are working-class Geordies and middle-class people living in Surrey respectively (Brah 1996: 17–18; emphasis added). To capture such experiences, simultaneously idiosyncratic and culturally shared, such 'modes of thinking and feeling', we may draw on Raymond Williams' notion of *structures of feeling*. The relevance of this idea to the study of ethnicity has been recognized by researchers interested in how 'ethnic claims and sentiments . . . are imprinted . . . in [both] our minds and bodies as patterns of ideas and sentiments' (Tambiah, quoted in Arnaut 2004: 115). In *Marxism and Literature*, Raymond Williams defines *structures of feeling* (1977: 132) as 'meanings and values as they are actively lived and felt . . . characteristic elements of impulse, restraint and tone; specifically affective elements of consciousness and relationships: not feeling against thought, but thought as felt and feeling as thought: practical consciousness of a present kind, in a living and inter-relating continuity'. Williams thus conceptualizes cultural consciousness as experienced and felt by situated, living human beings, as 'a kind of feeling and thinking which is . . . social and material' (1977: 131).

To illustrate the structured and culturally shared character of such feelings and consciousness, we turn to Caroline Moorehead's account of a Palestinian refugee's memories:

> I remember how we used to take our olives to the press . . . how I used to stand around with the others and we used to . . . joke. I remember the weddings . . . and how in the summer we used to dance. I remember the way the men sat together and talked and how . . . I used to sit with them, listening. I remember the way the richest man . . . always had coffee for visitors and how the women used to visit each other in their houses. . . . There, our houses were surrounded by our lands. Here, it is like a prison. The land we look out on is owned by others. There the . . . celebrations and burials were all part of our lives, and we all shared in them. Here, unemployment and stress has driven all that away.
>
> (Moorehead 2005: 201)

This account bears witness to the deep emotional salience of an individual's biographical recollections, to the experience of culture as lived, shared and felt. Moreover, it also ties in with a recurrent theme of this book: the *structures of feeling* captured here implicate a form of *reflexivity*; we may therefore wonder if it is the experience of crises – in this particular case the painful consequences of displacement and exile – that can lead to the self-conscious articulation of *structures of feeling* now considered to be under erosion or already lost. Drawing on Bourdieu (1977), we may then ask if once we become conscious of our simultaneously cultural and personal *structures of feeling*, culture has turned into ethnicity, *habitus/doxa* into discourse, and everyday life has undergone some important transformations. It is at this point that we turn our attention to our second key theme.

EVERYDAY LIFE

If ethnicity has turned out to be a concept in need of elaborate discussion, how about everyday life? At a first glance, a working definition may appear self-evident: everyday life, we may suggest, comprises people's regular activities and routine practices, the often taken-for-granted cultural fabric of their lives, daily rituals as well as life-cycle events, the organization of family life and domestic space, food, language and other signifying practices as much as educational and occupational biographies. Useful though this is, it is another working definition offering a mere springboard into considerably more complex debates. We begin to discern a more differentiated picture in David Morgan's discussion of the following three partly overlapping meanings: first, everyday life involves 'events and experiences that . . . happen to most people in the course of their lives', the 'social meanings' attached to birth, sexuality, sickness and death; second, everyday life refers to 'the regular, the repeated, the routine, the familiar, the quotidian, the banal, even the boring'; third, Morgan observes, the idea of everyday life can have normative connotations of 'the normal' (2004: 37–38) and thus simultaneously points to what is considered different, 'abnormal', 'deviant' or even 'pathological'. Clearly, there is much of sociological significance in these dimensions, which partly explains a long-standing tradition of interest – among sociologists, critical theorists and others – in how the everyday 'works', what it means to social actors, how it might change over time and how it relates to structures of power and inequality.

An early contribution to what is now a formidable body of research and theorizing is encountered in Erving Goffman's *The Presentation of Self in Everyday Life*. Goffman conceptualizes social life through a series of theatrical (or 'dramaturgical') metaphors, as a stage comprising public 'front regions' and more closely guarded 'back regions', and social roles as performed – usually with the complicity of others – and dedicated to constructing and maintaining a 'working consensus' or particular 'definition' of a given situation. Highly influential though Goffman's work has been (particularly his notion of 'impression management' by the 'performing self' in its role compliance), it has also been subject to a number of criticisms. Thus, Baert acknowledges Goffman's revelations of 'those trivial aspects of daily life which remain unnoticed . . . [but] are central to the production of social order . . . predictability . . . [and] agreement concerning the meaning of objects and actions'; however, he also queries Goffman's relevance to an understanding of the larger 'politico-strategic order' (Baert 1998: 81). In other words, the question arises if Goffman sufficiently engages with, let alone

criticizes, existing configurations of power, exclusion and exploitation, for which – one may argue – certain social roles are a mere
euphemism. Second, does Goffman – in claiming that 'the
unthinking ease with which performers consistently carry off . . .
standard-maintaining routines does not deny that a performance
has occurred, merely that participants have been aware of it'
(1990[1959]: 81) – underestimate social actors' capacity for
reflection and hence potential political challenges? Third, and
following on from this, does a preoccupation with the 'symbolic
order' overlook historical changes both to shared meanings and power
structures? It is these three interrelated criticisms that facilitate the
construction of an analytical framework for the everyday.

Power (and resistance)

A core dimension in most sociological analyses, power is usually
taken to reflect an individual's or group's ability to implement their
will and pursue their interests 'regardless of resistance' and with or
without intentionality (see Abercrombie *et al.* 1984: 192–193).
While a more elaborate conceptualization of power will be explored
in later chapters, our main question for now is how we might theorize
the intersection of power relations with everyday life. One possibility
has already been discussed: Anthony Giddens' theory of structuration
(1984), according to which the routine practices of ordinary social
actors – motivated by the attempt to maintain a predictable, anxiety-
controlling world – are crucially implicated in the reproduction of
existing social relations. While this accounts for much social practice
(Goffman has notably been a major source of influence on Giddens),
we are once again left to wonder about everyday activities that disrupt
ontological security and subvert political structures. For example,
how about life styles seen by their practitioners as alternatives to the
patriarchal family or the capitalist mode of production? How about
the (daily) circulation and consumption of discourses that challenge
environmental degradation or 'Fortress Europe'? Berger and Del
Negro capture such contrasting ideological orientations by observing
that the 'notion of everydayness is highly political': it 'may be
disparaged as the domain of tedious, uncreative repetition [and] a
place where power relations are mindlessly reproduced'; alternatively,

it 'may be viewed positively as a realm of authentic, productive labour and celebrated as a site of resistance' (Berger and Del Negro 2004: 12). In other words, everyday life may be 'ordinary', but it is not trivial: instead, it is politically charged and sociologically significant, either as a mechanism of social reproduction or as a domain of human creativity and ideological challenges.

Henri Lefebvre's analysis of *Everyday Life in the Modern World* leans heavily in the former interpretive direction, claiming to uncover the 'ideological structure' underpinning the 'dull routine, the ongoing go-to-work, pay-the-bills, homeward trudge of daily existence' (Wander 2002: vii–ix). Lefebvre's critical theory of Western post-war societies paints a picture of alienation, superficial relationships and anonymous (sub-)urban life. In a challenge to crude versions of economic determinism, he emphasizes and criticizes the role of the media and the 'terror of advertising' in what he terms the 'bureaucratic society of controlled consumption': contemporary capitalism requires compliant consumers, subject to the 'dual method of (ideological) *persuasion* and *compulsion* (punishment, laws and codes, courts . . . armed forces, police etc)'; stifling creativity and spontaneity and repressing (sexual) desire, much everyday life is defined by 'tedious tasks [and] humiliations', by a *misery* particularly acute for women and the working classes (Lefebvre 2002 [1971]: 144, 35; emphasis in original). However, Lefebvre also offers glimpses of utopian hope (2002 [1971]: 124, 190, 205), observations of encounters and meaningful conversations that promise to transcend the misery of everyday life, where desire is celebrated and a bygone creative power of the everyday re-emerges; he traces much of this revolutionary potential to the artistic quarters in some of the world's metropolitan cities.

The latter interpretive tradition, which regards the everyday as a domain of resistance and creativity, is widely associated with Michel De Certeau's two volumes of *The Practice of Everyday Life* (1984; De Certeau *et al.* 1998). According to De Certeau, social order and discipline are less effective and all-engulfing than is commonly assumed. His work, which I discuss in more detail in Chapter 2, is premised on the attempt to 'discover how an entire society resists being reduced to [discipline], what popular procedures (. . ."miniscule" and quotidian) manipulate [disciplinary] mechanisms and . . . evade them' (1984: xiv). De Certeau's analyses reveal the multiple *tactics* of resistance employed by the dominated and disenfranchised, whose pleasures of consumption and everyday practices – whether reading, cooking, talking to neighbours or 'walking in the city' – enable them to temporarily slip through the web of power that surrounds them.

The centrality of power in everyday life and its relevance to understanding ethnic/racial exclusions emerge from analyses of racism as simultaneously 'ideology, structure and process' that pervade, and intersect in, the everyday: Philomena Essed shows that racism is a self-interested ideological construction of different groups of people in relations of hierarchy and/or outright opposition to one another; it is also a structure of 'rules, laws and regulations' that define unequal access to resources; and, crucially, 'racism is a process because structures and ideologies do not exist outside the everyday practices through which they are created and confirmed' (Essed 1991: 43–44). Similarly, Gail Lewis observes that 'racialising culture is ordinary', a 'field of discourse and practice in which we are all imbricated', encountered in the home, 'the micro-practices of workplace relationships as much as the institutional policies of employers . . . [in the] practices of the self and imagination as much as those of the media [and] the academy' (2004: 121).

Turning to the second of three interrelated analytical dimensions, we may now ask how conscious people are of the consequences of their seemingly ordinary assumptions and everyday practices, of how the latter play a crucial role in the reproduction of micro- and macro-structures of power and inequality.

Reflexivity

Reflexivity refers to a person's capacity to have an experience, to be aware of it, to be aware of the fact that he or she may be 'the focus of another's experience' (Berger and Del Negro 2004: 91), and to be aware of the wider consequences of their experiences and actions. Thus defined, we may wonder about the role and extent of people's reflexivity in, for example, the following account in Alan Sillitoe's novel about working-class drudgery as experienced by Arthur Seaton in Nottingham in the 1950s:

> 'Arthur,' his father called, in a deadly menacing Monday-morning voice
> . . . 'when are yer goin' ter get up? Yer'll be late fer wok.' . . . Arthur took
> a half-empty fag-packet from the mantelpiece, his comb, a ten-shilling
> note and heap of coins that had survived the pubs [and] bookies'
> counters. . . . A mug of tea was needed, then back to the treadmill;
> Monday was always the worst; by Wednesday he was broken-in. . . .
> Despite the previous tone of his father's voice, Arthur found him sitting
> at the table happily sipping tea. . . . [He] looked up from his cup. 'Come
> on Arthur, you ain't got much time. It's ten past seven and we've both
> got to be on by half-past.'
>
> (Sillitoe 1994 [1958]: 24–25)

The author's reflexive engagement with everyday working-class life
may be taken as given. Projecting our sociological concern with
reflexivity on to his novel's characters, we may ask if Arthur and his
father differ not only in the degree of their discontent with their
work routines but also in the extent to which they reflect on the
conditions of, and consequences to, their lives. How far does such
reflexivity stretch? To the immediacy of a person's sacrifices and
deprivations or, beyond that, to the capitalist relations of production
that define Arthur's and his family's lives? And how would we know?

Whatever the answer to these questions, reflexivity and – arguably
more frequently – its absence have been a defining concern
for sociologists of everyday life. This emerged most famously from
Harold Garfinkel's micro-sociological (*ethnomethodological*) 'breach
experiments' that involved, for example, asking students to behave as
though they were boarders rather than family members in their
households. The bewilderment, anxiety and annoyance triggered by
such experiments revealed the fragility of social relations that require
the constant collaborative performance and maintenance of a
background of 'seen but unnoticed' common understandings; from
an ethnomethodological perspective, social life is and remains
meaningful thanks to the 'ongoing accomplishments of organized
. . . practices of everyday life'; yet most people most of the time remain
unaware of their own role in the skilful creation and reproduction of
social order, its 'routinized character' and their shared expectancies
and 'background of relevances [that are] simply "there" and taken for
granted' (Garfinkel 2004 [1967]: 44–53, 118). Like Goffman,

Garfinkel has been criticized for neglecting asymmetrical power relations and possible 'transformations in the underlying social structure' (Baert 1998: 88). It is here that our three dimensions for understanding the everyday intersect most clearly: when confronted by structures of inequality and experiences of marginalization, can we really assume that 'background expectancies' remain unnoticed and unproblematized? Alternatively, can growing reflexivity not give rise to political challenges and hence social change? As mentioned earlier, there is a strand in the study of everyday life that insists on its creative, revolutionary, utopian potential. The question to be raised now and to be pursued in due course is this: Are such challenges to the status quo, born of reflexivity and hence increasing awareness of the wider contexts and consequences of our everyday lives, mainly encountered in the writings of cultural theorists and the signifying practices of avant-garde artists (see Gardiner 2000)? How about reflexivity giving rise to acts of (everyday) resistance in more mundane settings, among people like Arthur Seaton? Turning to our third analytical dimension, we may further wonder if reflexivity is for many of us, rather than the exception to the rule, a defining characteristic of the current historical era.

History

Do the characteristics of everyday life vary according to historical context? The obvious answer would be yes, of course they do; yet there has been considerable sociological debate on how and why they differ. The above-mentioned Henri Lefebvre insists on the historical specificity of the everyday misery he describes and criticizes: it is a modern phenomenon, specific to a particular stage in capitalist development, characteristic of a social formation defined by bureaucratically imposed and controlled consumption; as such, according to Lefebvre, it stands in contrast to the alleged authenticity of peasant societies, to the 'style' and 'festival' of earlier historical periods; moreover, there is the hope that a 'permanent cultural revolution' may yet liberate human desires and transform everyday life into a domain of art, play and meaningful interaction (2002 [1971]: 36, 200–206).

However, it is not only authors explicitly concerned with the concept of the everyday who have debated its historically variable characteristics. Indeed, do not most sociological theories in some way address and attempt to illuminate everyday lives, their conditions and consequences? And is not all such theorizing by necessity conscious of historical context and change? Pre-empting a body of work to be discussed in later chapters, we may consider Zygmunt Bauman's wide-ranging analyses (2000, 2003, 2005) of what he terms *liquid modernity*: this is a novel social condition, in which people's everyday lives are no longer shaped by the work ethic and a relatively stable position in industrialized societies but, instead, by the forces and consequences of globalization, the practices of consumerism, new forms of inequality and exclusion, as well as by the psychological and interpersonal consequences of a climate of chronic uncertainty, atomizing individualism and instability. Even more relevant for our present purposes is Anthony Giddens' seminal analysis of *Modernity and Self-identity* (1991). The current 'late modern age' is, Giddens argues, defined by a series of transformations affecting day-to-day life and closely associated with a dialectic between global forces and local experiences. In contrast to pre-modern societies, tradition has now lost much of its self-evident character as a source of authority and ontological security, and as a framework for social action. The symptoms of late modernity include the emergence of the 'pure relationship' (motivated by individuals' quest for emotional satisfaction rather than cultural expectations and norms), the heightened significance of the body as a source of self-definition (or 'self-actualization' in Giddens' terminology), and 'life politics'. In contrast to the 'emancipatory politics' of yester-year, life politics is concerned with life styles rather than with life chances (Giddens 1991: 214). The lowest common denominator underpinning these varied manifestations of late modernity is what Giddens terms its 'extreme reflexivity':

> [E]veryone is . . . aware of the reflexive constitution of modern social activity and the implications it has for her or his life. Self-identity for us forms a *trajectory* across the different institutional settings of modernity over the *dur e* of . . . the 'life cycle' . . . Each of us not only 'has', but *lives* a biography reflexively organised in terms of . . . possible ways of life.

> Modernity is a post-traditional order, in which the question, 'How shall
> I live?' has to be answered in day-to-day decisions about how to behave,
> what to wear and what to eat – and many other things.
>
> (Giddens 1991: 14, italics in the original)

The key issues addressed in our case studies include the questions as
to how ethnicity fares under the social conditions of late or liquid
modernity, how individuals negotiate ethnic identities and cultural
traditions in their more or less reflexively organized biographies,
how such continuous processes unfold in the context of their everyday
lives, and to the backdrop of historically novel forms of exclusion
and uncertainty.

CONCLUSION

We have covered a lot of ground in this chapter. Following a brief
discussion of some conceptual overlaps between the notions of
ethnicity, nations and 'races', we revisited a classic debate concerning
the 'hold' which ethnicity exercises over individuals or, conversely,
the scope of agency in appropriating, negotiating and possibly
resisting cultural traditions and expectations. This was followed by
a discussion of the relationship between culture (itself a concept
that requires considerable thought and careful conceptualization)
and ethnicity. I then established multi-dimensional analytical
frameworks for our two key concepts. I argued that ethnicity is best
regarded as simultaneously a set of structures that both constrain
and enable social action, as a *way of seeing* the world, and as
biographically grounded *structures of feeling*. In order to get a
sociological handle on everyday life, I suggested that we need to
think about power and resistance, reflexivity and/or a lack thereof,
and the historical specificity and variability of the everyday.
Importantly, these various dimensions need to be thought of as
interrelated.

The case studies that follow explore the interplay of ethnicity and
everyday life thus conceptualized in various empirical settings which
happen to constitute my areas of research interest. It goes without
saying that any number of other historical, geographical and cultural
settings could serve as at least equally illuminating case studies. In

addition, constraints of space require a careful selection of conceptual foci in each of the following chapters: Chapter 2 examines questions of power and resistance, Chapter 3 focuses on the notion of 'identity', Chapter 4 returns to the issue of reflexivity, and Chapter 5 is preoccupied with historical contexts. Crucially, however, the various empirical settings examined would – of course – have equally allowed for other configurations: power and resistance are of crucial relevance in each context, as are identities, reflexivity (or its absence) and historical changes. Rather than providing complete analyses, the following chapters must therefore be seen as mere snapshots selected to draw attention to particular aspects of the always far more complex intersection of ethnicity and everyday life.

Before concluding this chapter, we should briefly address questions of a methodological nature, including how and by whom ethnicity and everyday life are studied. I have so far made use of work originating in a number of cognate disciplines, including sociology but also cultural studies, social anthropology, political science and history. The eclectic use of findings generated by scholars who often work with different though complementary methods – including semi-/unstructured interviews, participant observation, documentary and media analyses, biographical methods and others – will continue throughout this book and, as such, warrants an explanatory note. The sociology of ethnicity and everyday life advocated in the following pages will, in particular, be complemented by social anthropological and social historical data.

Traditionally the study of pre-industrial, non-Western societies, social anthropology's concerns include our two core ideas – culture/ethnicity and the everyday. In the course of long-term ethnographic fieldwork anthropologists live with their informants, learn to speak their language, participate in their rituals and strive to understand their worldview. While anthropological findings are therefore clearly relevant to our discussion, we may suggest that a distinctly sociological approach to ethnicity and everyday life exhibits the following characteristics among others: first, the observation that ethnicity and culture are not identical, that it is the politicization of culture which gives rise to ethnicity (see above); second, the discipline's preoccupation with modern, (post-)industrial societies and its own theoretical traditions (e.g. Malešević 2004).

However, this difference is not absolute. Anthropology has been observed to have 'come home' and sociologists have studied non-Western societies. In theoretical terms, many of the models and analyses discussed thus far are associated with sociologists, though certainly not all of them are. The study of ethnicity and everyday life is thus by definition an interdisciplinary endeavour and engagement across disciplinary boundaries is mutually beneficial.

A similar case may be made for dialogue between sociologists and (social) historians with a shared interest in the significance of culture/ethnicity in people's 'ordinary lives'. I have already argued that the sociological study of everyday ethnicity needs to engage with history in an even more fundamental sense by addressing two interrelated issues: first, the question if and how the experience of ethnicity in everyday life varies between different historical eras; second, specific questions concerning the significance of everyday ethnicity at the beginning of the twenty-first century. In other words, the sociology of ethnicity and everyday life needs to be 'historicized'. It is a core assumption underpinning this book that such an endeavour is at its most illuminating when grounded in a proud tradition of sociological research and theorizing while simultaneously being open to interdisciplinary work and borrowings.

Furthermore, academics (regardless of their disciplinary orientations) do not hold a monopoly on research and reflections on ethnicity and everyday life. To assume that they do would blind us to some highly revealing sources of data. The material examined in what follows therefore reflects an attempt to cast a sociological eye over a wide variety of writings, ranging from academic work to investigative journalism, newspapers and life-style magazines, from popular music to novels and other forms of cultural signifying practices. In analysing such different sources we must of course be acutely aware of important differences between discourses and genres. We must ask ourselves questions about the author's (i.e. any author's) interests, assumptions and intended audiences; we must ask ourselves whether any given representation provides a description or analysis (and how it does either), what alternative accounts there are, and why they might differ. We must differentiate between reasoned, (relatively) detached analysis and data that form part of the social field under investigation; the latter may include vastly different statements, narratives and activities that provide insights into ethnicity in everyday life and can therefore enrich our ensuing sociological analyses.

To illustrate the value of interdisciplinary borrowings and of the use of a wide variety of data, I would like to conclude this chapter by briefly commenting on what is simultaneously a tremendously important historical document and part of the canon of great twentieth-century writing: Anne Frank's *The Diary of a Young Girl*. Written during her years of hiding in an Amsterdam annexe, Anne's heart-breaking diary reveals much about the suffering of millions at the hands of the Nazi machinery of hatred and genocide; moreover, Anne's diary captures significant aspects of the universal human condition – love and longing, the trials of growing up, passion, solidarity and hope (against hope as it was to so tragically unfold). In other words, Anne's diary captures what was historically specific about the horrors of the Holocaust; beyond that, Anne also reminds us of what is common to all of us. Her reflections on her everyday life in the annexe also bring to light an extreme version of a set of processes in which many discourses of ethnic belonging are implicated: the external imposition of labels and social positions by powerful outsiders, insiders' (partial) identification with 'the group', as well as possible incongruities between ascribed identities and the everyday practices and real lives of the individuals thus designated.

The first emerges with particular clarity from Anne's early recordings (2000: 8) of her German Jewish relatives' suffering under Hitler's anti-Jewish laws and their escape into exile, the German invasion of Holland and, subsequently, the everyday segregation and deprivations imposed by the Nazi anti-Jewish decrees; as we now know, these were the first manifestations of an institutional willingness and ability to confine – with unparalleled ferocity – millions into a particular social category that led to the death camps and Anne's own tragic death in Bergen-Belsen in early 1945. Near the end of her time in hiding, Anne reflected thus:

> We've been strongly reminded . . . that we're Jews in chains . . . without any rights, but with a thousand obligations. . . . One day this terrible war will be over . . . when we'll be people again and not just Jews! Who has inflicted this on us? Who has set us apart from all the rest? Who has put

us through such suffering? . . . We can never be just Dutch, or just English
. . . we will always be Jews as well . . . but then, we'll want to be. . . .
Through the ages Jews have had to suffer, but through the ages they've
gone on living.

(Frank 2000: 260)

Clearly, Anne identifies here with the Jewish people, its history of
exclusion and suffering; however, she also makes it clear that
identities can be multi-dimensional: in the same diary entry, on 11
April 1944, she goes on to say that her 'first wish after the war is to
become a Dutch citizen'. A few months earlier she wondered 'if
anyone will ever . . . not worry about whether or not I'm Jewish and
merely see me as a teenager in need of some good plain fun' (2000:
153). Anne shows that identities in fact are not unitary, that real,
everyday lives and people's biographies cannot even in the darkest
of times be confined to one side of an arbitrary ideological boundary:
Anne thus also tells us of her first-ever Christmas present, that her
father wrote his poems only in German, and of an incident when she
herself had articulated her upset (about an accident resulting in her
schoolwork being soaked) in German (2000: 155, 106, 297).

Anne Frank's tragically short life holds many lessons for us all to
learn; her life was defined by powerful outsiders' ability to define
her, her family and millions deemed to be 'like them'; written in the
darkest and most murderous of circumstances, her diary shows that
ethnicity also crucially involves self-identifying individuals, and that
identities can remain ambivalent and contestable; moreover, Anne's
diary reveals everyday life to be highly political, to allow for human
creativity and reflexivity, and – most of all – to be profoundly shaped
by historical contexts.

2

POWER AND CLASSIFICATION, MEANING AND RESISTANCE

This chapter explores a defining characteristic of ethnicity: ethnic communities and identities rely on social processes of classification that simultaneously include some people and exclude others, and hence construct and reproduce social boundaries. Such boundary maintenance constitutes a form of both political and symbolic practice: it is profoundly political insofar as the construction and reproduction of ethnic identities needs to be understood in its wider contexts of unequally distributed power; and it is symbolic insofar as it makes use of repertoires of culturally shared meaning. Richard Jenkins, whose *Rethinking Ethnicity* (1997) will frame the discussion in this chapter, develops a crucial distinction that goes some way towards illuminating this two-sided process constitutive of ethnic identities. He distinguishes between *social categorization* and *group identification*: social categorization refers to acts of 'external definition' and processes of labelling by institutions and social actors with 'sufficient power and authority' to impose their classifications and allocate individuals to particular groupings (Jenkins 1997: 80); group identification, on the other hand, is a group-internal process, whereby individuals define themselves and others as belonging to the same community, make more or less conscious use of shared meaning, and profess experiences of collective 'belonging'. Jenkins (1997: 23) emphasizes that though the two phenomena are 'inextricably linked', they constitute 'two analytically distinct processes of ascription': while social categorization captures the impact of powerful outsiders on (the construction and/or reification of) ethnic groups, group identification refers to the shared experience of cultural meaning, history and solidarity.

In this chapter, I explore some of the ways in which external power, through different means that include social classification, impacts on a range of communities variously identified as 'Travellers', Romani or 'Gypsy-Travellers'. In doing so, I focus on the literature on UK Travellers but also make use of some illuminating studies of Roma communities in Central and Eastern Europe since the collapse of communism. Moreover, I examine existing evidence of group identification and symbolic resistance (against sedentary power) within Traveller communities. Crucially, the following analysis emphasizes that both external power and internal group identification directly affect – and take place within – the realm of everyday life. I argue that an understanding of the everyday among Travellers benefits from an engagement with relevant sociological theories of power and resistance. Such an engagement illuminates both external power exercised *on* and internal power exercised *within* ethnic communities.

HISTORY, EXCLUSION, CULTURE

The recent academic literature on Romani/'Gypsy-Traveller' communities exhibits a tension between two competing paradigms. The historically dominant strand argues that there are crucial commonalities among globally dispersed groups comprising some twelve million people, whose origins can be traced to India. Ian Hancock, a prominent exponent of this school of thought, observes that 'everywhere in Europe, throughout North and South America and Australia, as well as in parts of Africa and Asia, there are found people who refer to themselves as Romani . . . [who] maintain a language and a culture which set them quite apart from the rest of the world' (2002: 1) and whose presence in Europe was first recorded in the late thirteenth century. Hancock records linguistic similarities between Romani and Sanskrit as well as cultural parallels with northwestern India, which point to the Romanies' South Asian origins and trace the beginnings of (some of) their ancestors' westward migration to some time after the year 1000.

A very different interpretation has been proposed by Brian Belton who shifts the focus from questions of descent and common culture towards wider structural and historical factors that have enabled the construction of the ethnic label 'Gypsy'. The latter, according to Belton, wrongly homogenizes a huge diversity of people, for whom there is 'little to suggest that [they] can be seen as an ethnic, racial, biological or historical whole' (2005: 93). Belton's 'new paradigm' holds instead that it is in social interaction and with the help of explanatory, meaning-making 'ethnic narratives' (analogous to my earlier discussion of ethnicity as a *way of seeing*) that the category of 'the Gypsy' is created, imposed and often internalized by those labelled as such. This interpretation corroborates the significance of the two separate yet interrelated processes of external social classification and internal group identification emphasized by Jenkins. Moreover, Belton analyses the wider historical contexts within which the imposition and appropriation of socially constructed ethnic categories takes place: Gypsy identities, Belton argues (2005: 154–163), have emerged through legislation 'aimed at promoting market . . . norms' and hence in the institutional nexus of capitalist societies that cannot tolerate deviation from their logic of sedentary housing and waged employment.

These very different approaches emphasize cultural factors (i.e. language, ritual practices, taken-for-granted worldviews) and structural 'locations' (i.e. people's different positions in relations of power and inequality) informing Traveller ethnicity respectively. As this discussion will show, there are important truths in both; the challenge therefore lies in reconciling cultural commonalities and continuities with great internal diversity, and the wider historical and political contexts in which Traveller identities are constructed, experienced, articulated and negotiated. Belton rightly and importantly emphasizes that cultural and individual heterogeneities are unhelpfully denied and strategically overlooked by rigid social categories imposed in wider fields of power and exclusion (though, as we shall see, this has not been the exclusive property of capitalist social formations). However, this cannot detract from the equally important observation that culturally shared and transmitted ideas, practices and traditions matter greatly to many self-identifying 'Gypsies'. Social classification and group identification, external and internal power as well as possible resistance, historically and geographically specific socio-economic structures, cultural traditions and discourses of ethnic membership all intersect in the everyday lives of individuals designated by themselves and others as 'Gypsy-Travellers'.

The literature on the narrower British context confirms that there are very considerable diversities within the broad category of 'Travellers'. A common typology distinguishes between partly Romani-speaking English and Welsh 'Gypsies', partly 'Cant'-speaking Scottish Travellers, and partly Shelta-speaking (a language of Celtic origins) Irish Travellers (e.g. Barnes 1975: 232). Significant socio-economic stratification among Travellers (e.g. Okely 1975; Hawes and Perez 1995; Mac Laughlin 1999), reflected in differences in wealth, property and migratory patterns (if any), further challenges the homogenizing and misleading stereotype of the exotic, invariably nomadic and inevitably poverty-stricken 'Gypsy other'. Moreover, in spite of cultural preferences for ethnic endogamy (i.e. marriage within the group) and a (semi-)nomadic life style, Traveller history has included some intermarriage, settlement and/or assimilation to sedentary society. It is for these reasons that Judith Okely (1983) has suggested that what the heterogeneous groups often subsumed under the 'Traveller-Gypsy' label share is best described as an 'ethnic ideology' and its manifold symbolic and everyday expression: this is a worldview emphasizing the significance of descent, self-employment, the ideal (though only a regular practice among certain sections) of (semi-)nomadism, and the identity-bestowing distinction of the 'Gypsy self' from the 'non-Gypsy' (*gorgio* or *gaujo*) 'other' (see below). While often resisting pressures to assimilate to the sedentary and 'proletarianized' way of life, Travellers are reliant on the dominant social order and 'can only survive . . . [in] the context of the larger economy . . . within which they exploit geographical mobility and a multiplicity of occupations' (Okely 1983: 30). Such economic adaptability manifests in a range of 'traditional' pursuits including seasonal agricultural labour, the selling of pegs, flowers and lace, fortune telling and fairground work, as well as in more 'modern' niches such as 'scrap dealing (or metal recycling), tarmacing . . . dealing in second-hand cars, garden clearance and tree felling' (www.slamnet. org.uk/traveller_communities.html, 18 July 2003).

This summary suggests that Travellers' ethnicity and everyday lives are indeed shaped by both cultural and structural characteristics: while the former are encountered in certain traditional practices and ideas of belonging and difference, the latter concern experiences of social exclusion and economic marginality shared with other groups including the widely demonized 'New Age Travellers' (Sibley 1997: 228) as well as 'Fairground Travellers, or Showmen' (Kiddle 1999: 96). As already indicated, our discussion needs to account for both cultural and structural features. We turn to the latter first.

CLASSIFICATION AND SURVEILLANCE

Romani history has been partly defined by different forms of exclusion, persecution, oppression and marginalization at the hands of others: from centuries of enslavement in parts of the Ottoman Empire (Hancock 2002: 16–28), policies of compulsory settlement by the Habsburg Empress Maria Theresa in the eighteenth century (Bancroft 2005: 27), Romanies' inclusion in the category of people deemed 'subhuman' by the Nazis and murdered in the death camps (e.g. Pogány 2004: 35–47), to a renewed period of enforced assimilation under state communism in Central and Eastern Europe in the second half of the twentieth century (e.g. Scheffel 2005). The recurring denominators spanning historical eras and geographical areas have been the construction of Romanies/Gypsy-Travellers as the 'other' by powerful outsiders and Travellers' being subject to external political authorities, methods of control or expulsion. Limiting his historical focus to the modern period, Bancroft (2005: 149–150) distinguishes between two strategies that are applied – sometimes in combination – by nation states to communities considered to be outsiders: on the one hand, coercive integration implying the erasure of signs of cultural difference; and, on the other, the permanent removal, separation and ghettoization of 'the other'; we shall see in later chapters that these often co-existing 'alternatives' of enforced assimilation and expulsion have not only been applied to Romanies but indeed define the relationship between many states and various groups seen as ethnic strangers. Within the yet narrower historical framework of the contemporary era (i.e. the period since the collapse of communism and the end of the Cold War in 1989), Roma and

Gypsy-Travellers have found themselves, once again, pushed to and beyond the margins of many of the societies they have often lived in for centuries. In particular in parts of Central and Eastern Europe, they are experiencing renewed racist violence, discrimination by local authorities, chronic unemployment, poverty and the physical separation (in barely habitable ghettos) from their local, non-Roma neighbours (e.g. Bancroft 1999, 2005; Pogány 2004; Scheffel 2005). While these may be the most extreme contemporary forms of exclusion inflicted upon Romanies, it has been pointed out that Gypsy-Travellers are also among the most vilified and marginalized of all minority communities in many Western democracies (e.g. Hancock 1997). This raises questions we shall concentrate on in this section: How have Gypsy-Travellers in the UK fared over recent decades? How have local/national politics and legislative changes impacted on their everyday lives? And are there relevant (sociological) theories that facilitate analysis (and possible criticism) of this?

Recent literature on Gypsy-Travellers (e.g. Karner 2004b; Bancroft 2005; Belton 2005) has discovered the relevance of Michel Foucault's various analyses of modern power. In *Discipline and Punish* (1991 [1975]), Foucault argues that the rise of modernity towards the end of the eighteenth century saw the emergence of a new institutional logic that came to define the operations of prisons, schools, hospitals, factories and armies alike: a logic of one-way surveillance, in which inmates, workers, patients, pupils and soldiers knew themselves to be under the gaze of authority and as a result of which they policed themselves and their increasingly 'docile bodies' into discipline. Foucault saw this new mechanism of social control epitomized in Jeremy Bentham's design of the panoptical prison: structured around a central inspection tower, every inmate's cell was now constantly and entirely visible – without, however, the watched being able to see their observers. The pervasiveness of this historically novel model of surveillance, control and normalization leads Foucault to speak of the modern 'carceral network' based on a range of panoptical institutions and concomitant forms of knowledge about the individual.

The effects of modern power on Travellers are stressed by Mac Laughlin who writes of 'a new geography of power and surveillance

. . . a new moral education, and . . . extended administrative control over the timing and spacing of human activities' (1999: 141). Sibley similarly refers to a number of social control agencies including 'teachers, social workers, police and local government officers . . . who impinge on the economic and social life of outsiders' (1981: 21). Indeed, certain key legislative changes in the second half of the twentieth century yield themselves to a Foucauldian reading. The 1968 Caravan Sites Act obligated local authorities to provide sufficient sites for 'the numbers of Gypsies and Travellers . . . in the area' (Hawes and Perez 1995: 22). Compared to the previous 1960 Caravan Sites and Development Act, which had introduced (hard-to-obtain) planning permissions and sites licences as legal requirements for caravans to be parked on private land, the 1968 Act was widely seen as an achievement of liberal politics (see Bancroft 2005: 85). However, it has also been criticized: first, for sometimes under-estimating the numbers of local Travellers; second, for its arguably assimilationist sub-text that ultimately intended for Travellers to settle (e.g. Sibley 1981: 95; Okely 1983: 111). Once it was deemed that 'sufficient site provision' had been made, councils could apply for 'designations', which – if granted – empowered them to evict Travellers from unauthorized sites and hence to arguably criminalize nonconformist patterns of migration and stopping. In addition, 'district councils . . . were to be responsible for the management of sites' (Hawes and Perez 1995: 23) thus enabling them to control space, access to land and the running of sites, all of which are crucial in Travellers' (everyday) lives. Most revealing, however, was the planned spatial design of the new sites: the Act included a 'design for a gypsy trailer site' (Sibley 1981: 32), which envisaged a rectangular area symmetrically subdivided into an even number of 'cells' each consisting of four 30-foot x 10-foot caravan 'standings', a toilet block per cell and one scrap compound and recreation area per site. This has led Sibley to argue that such 'Cartesian geometry in environmental design . . . [forms] the stock response of authority to non-conforming minorities judged to be deviant' (1981: 31) and often contravenes their own cultural preferences in the organization of space (see Okely 1983: 88). Crucially, the official site design fitted Foucault's panoptic schema: strategically placed street lights and, importantly, a warden's block and office made surveillance more efficient and potentially constant.

The 'carceral network' of modernity operates, Foucault argues further, according to 'the seven universal maxims of the good penitential condition': correction, classification, modulation, work, education, technical supervision and auxiliary institutions (1991 [1975]: 269). Given the arguably assimilationist intentions, official site management and the formation of county council liaison groups and officers, the principles of correction, technical supervision and auxiliary institutions were part of the implementation of the 1968 Act. Moreover, semi-permanent settlement in officially designated locations illustrates the impact of sedentary powers on Travellers' everyday lives, particularly in facilitating the more efficient control of their work and the provision of education. However, it is the maxim of classification that appears to be the most fundamental in Foucault's model (also see Belton 2005). The 1968 Act was careful to define, and hence classify, who was to be targeted by the new provision – 'persons of nomadic habit, whatever their race or origin', though excluding travelling showmen (Kiddle 1999: 25). Purportedly based on non-ethnic 'markers', the Act therefore defined a nomadic way of life as the criterion of inclusion in the new category of official caravan-site dwellers. Classification also further entailed modulation – the person/group-specific 'treatment' of, or response to, the subjects constructed in the act of categorization. Put another way, the 1968 Act defined a particular category of people, those 'of nomadic habit', as the (only) legitimate inhabitants of the sites to be managed by local authorities.

Following the introduction of the 1994 Criminal Justice and Public Order Act, many Travellers' lives deteriorated considerably. Directed mainly at the 'spatial transgressions' widely associated with New Age Travellers, the 1994 Act repealed the site provision measures enforced by the 1968 Act (e.g. Bancroft 2005: 84). It thereby further increased assimilationist pressures on Gypsy-Travellers and frequently contributed to exacerbating tensions between Travellers and local authorities as well as 'sedentary neighbours' (e.g. BBC 3: 28 September 2005). This has led several commentators to argue that Travellers have been 'pathologized' (Bancroft 2005: 78) and 'criminalized' (e.g. Halfacree 1996):

> As a result of the Act, Gypsy-Travellers were forced to move around more frequently . . . by the authorities. . . . In removing the rights of Gypsy-Travellers under the 1968 Act the Major government attacked the politically weakest section of British society. Council site building ground to a halt at the same time as it became much more difficult . . . to get planning permission for private sites. The Act became unworkable in practice because there was quite often literally nowhere for them to go . . . [and] led to greater numbers of roadside sites.
>
> (Bancroft 2005: 90, 92)

The detrimental effects of the 1994 Act on Travellers' (everyday) lives are obvious. In sociological terms we may wonder if the timing of this piece of legislation can be related to its wider historical context: does the contemporary form of social exclusion suffered by Gypsy-Travellers take a postmodern (and post-panoptical) form? Can this be related to processes of globalization?

Despite the above-mentioned criticisms of the 1968 Act, the period following its implementation has also been described as an 'era of consensus' (Hawes and Perez 1995). In removing the requirement to build sites for local Gypsy-Travellers, was the 1994 Act – we may ask – indicative of a new system of social exclusion? In different parts of his wide-ranging analyses, Zygmunt Bauman (1992, 2005) argues that contemporary post- or liquid modernity achieves social order primarily through 'consumerist seduction' – things work as long as, and because, we consume. However, Bauman also observes that there is a new 'underclass', so-called 'flawed consumers', who are either still subject to 'panoptical repression' or, increasingly, permanent exclusion (or indeed both). Travellers' ideological preference for semi-nomadism, if only as an ideal and a possibility, threatens to subvert panoptic surveillance. It is therefore also worth noting that the 1994 Act removed 'all rights for Gypsy-Travellers to stop anywhere but on authorized site[s]' (Bancroft 2005: 90), which were no longer a legal requirement for councils to build and some of which, as we saw, incorporated elements of panoptic control. At the same time, widespread (though not universal) economic hardship and the spatial limitations of caravan living put limits on Gypsy-Travellers' consumption potential (Kiddle 1999: 38) and hence position them on the periphery of consumer societies. The latter are, according to

Bauman, also increasingly at the mercy of multinational corporations: perhaps ironically, theirs is a very different and hugely consequential form of nomadism, which allows them to relocate to wherever production costs are deemed to be lowest. As a result, nation states and localities are having to compete to attract global capital. Bancroft illustrates how this can directly affect Traveller communities in documenting the case of a local authority clearing Travellers' horses from council-owned land that was 'earmarked as . . . a potential business site'; in times of globalization, then, 'as localities are increasingly . . . compet[ing] . . . in a global marketplace they seek to exclude groups who might impact on their competitive ability' (Bancroft 2005: 128–129, 145). The emerging picture of Gypsy-Travellers' contemporary exclusion is rounded off by a recent analysis of how old 'anti-Gypsy' prejudice is overlaid by contemporary anxieties about crime and 'the underclass' with which Travellers are associated in much media discourse (Vanderbeck 2003).

The discussion in this section has focused on some of the ways in which Travellers have been labelled and categorized by powerful outsiders. As such, it has addressed the first of the two key dimensions of ethnicity emphasized by Richard Jenkins: social classification. However, we have also seen that classification is only ever a part of, or precursor to, various political practices of control, assimilation, exclusion or stigmatization imposed on, and experienced by, Travellers. We now turn to the second dimension – group identification. In doing so, we examine aspects of cultural resistance.

RESISTANCE AND THE EVERYDAY

The operation of mechanisms of power does not guarantee their effectiveness. Classification, which is integral to the fabrication of disciplined subjects and a key characteristic of ethnicity according to Foucault and Jenkins respectively, can be contested. For example, 'Anglo-Roma Gypsies' and 'Irish Travellers' were recognized as ethnic minorities under the 1976 Race Relations Act. However, an organization called 'Friends, Families and Travellers' rejects the arbitrary exclusion of Scottish and New Age Travellers from this official definition:

> We feel that being a Traveller is [largely] a matter of personal definition. We do not feel it is right to [discount] someone's Traveller identity because they have settled. Equally, we do not believe it is right to refuse [to acknowledge] someone as a Traveller because they do not come from a long history of Travellers. . . . [T]he right to be a Traveller is the right to a way of life . . . a basic human right equal to all.
>
> (www.groundswelluk.net/~fft.htm, 2 July 2003)

Contesting official systems of classification is thus one form of resistance against sedentary power. In this section, I return to some of the above-mentioned cultural factors – shared ideas, discourses of belonging, social organization, historically grounded ways of doing things – that shape some Travellers' everyday lives and, crucially, constitute other forms of resisting dominant, external, and often encroaching structures of power. In theoretical terms, I argue that Michel De Certeau's analyses of *The Practice of Everyday Life* provide a useful framework for conceptualizing and understanding a more or less widely shared cultural universe of meaning, social action and resistance. De Certeau's two volumes (1984; De Certeau *et al.* 1998) investigate the seemingly mundane practices of consumers, readers, inhabitants of urban neighbourhoods and, most famously, pedestrians 'walking in the city' as *tactics* employed by the relatively weak to slip – if only temporarily – through the web of power, in which they are embedded. Everyday practice, Certeau argues, uses ideas and commodities provided by the dominant socio-economic order in indeterminate ways, allowing for the construction of autonomous meaning, the exercise of agency and the possibility of symbolic resistance. Although De Certeau uses very different case studies, his theoretical insights provide a way of understanding some Gypsy-Travellers' cultural practices as means of both 'group identification' (Jenkins 1997) and everyday resistance to external power.

We saw in Chapter 1 that historical context, power and resistance are among the key dimensions for a sociological understanding of everyday life. While the above section provided insights into the effects of powerful outsiders on Travellers in changing historical contexts, this section examines forms of symbolic resistance enacted by Travellers. Drawing on a seminal ethnographic study (Okely

1983), we also return to two of the key characteristics of ethnicity discussed in the previous chapter: the cultural ideas and practices discussed here reflect both *ways of seeing* the world and *structures of action* that make certain practices more likely than others and in so doing help reproduce existing social relationships that partly define the ethnic community.

According to Judith Okely (1983), the crucial characteristic of Travellers' 'ethnic ideology' is the symbolic boundary maintenance between the 'Gypsy self' and the non-Gypsy or 'Gorgio other'. While Okely emphasizes that Travellers' structural marginality provides the inescapable context to their discourse of identity and difference, she devotes much of her work to recording and analysing the many symbolic and ritual expressions of the Gypsy/Gorgio dichotomy. The perhaps clearest illustration of a cultural logic based on the strict separation of the categories of 'self' and 'other' is provided by ideas of purity and pollution: Okely shows that the insides of camps, trailers and bodies all symbolize the ethnic self, which is kept strictly separate from, and hence symbolically uncontaminated by, the outside that signifies sedentary, Gorgio society. Every contact between insides and outsides, every blurring of the inside/outside boundary are sources of symbolic danger and pollution that are ritualistically guarded against; hence the pronounced cultural preference for endogamy (i.e. marriage within the group) and Travellers' rituals of cleanliness: the latter, Okely shows, emphasize the importance of keeping the insides of trailers spotless (while little regard may be paid to the outside), of using different bowls for washing eating utensils (which come in contact with the inner body that is symbolic of the self) and clothes/body parts (which are in constant danger of pollution through contact with outsiders) respectively. Biological processes, including birth, death and menstruation, in which parts of 'the inside come outside' (Okely 1983: 211), are seen as other sources of danger and pollution. The same logic of ethnic boundary maintenance underlies Travellers' construction of cats and other animals that lick their fur, thus ignoring the symbolic boundary separating the inside from the outside, as unclean. Conversely, the hedgehog whose prickly exterior keeps that boundary clear and intact is considered to be clean and hence held in high cultural esteem (Okely 1983: 91–101).

Two aspects of Michel De Certeau's theoretical edifice advance the analysis of Traveller-Gypsies' symbolisms of difference. First, De Certeau argues that every legal and/or socio-economic system is 'inscribed on bodies', articulates itself through bodies and hence makes the individual 'body tell the code' (1984: 148). In other words, bodies are treated as signs, they symbolize – or literally embody – a social and cultural order. This resonates with Okely's findings concerning Travellers' symbolic universe, in which bodies play a central role: the symbolic separation (or confusion) of inner and outer bodies informs notions of cleanliness (or pollution), the structuring of space, and the cultural distinction between clean and unclean animals (depending on their bodily characteristics and behaviours). As Okely confirms, such bodily symbolisms are for many Travellers crucial ways of 'draw[ing] boundaries between themselves and Gorgios' (1983: 103). Put another way, the De Certeau-ian transformation of 'bodies into signs' here spells out an alternative cultural order, ethnically specific *ways of seeing* and acting in the world that resist being absorbed by the Gorgio, sedentary system.

De Certeau provides a second conceptual insight applicable to Travellers. Regarding the modalities of power and resistance, he contrasts *strategies* with *tactics*. He associates strategies with domination and defines them as 'possible when a subject of will and power (a proprietor, an enterprise, a city, a scientific institution) can be isolated . . . [and possesses] a place . . . serving as the basis for generating relations with an exterior' (1984: xix). Tactics, on the other hand, can rely on no such 'spatial or institutional localization' serving as a power base. Thus operating on territory controlled by the powerful other, tactics 'manipulate time' within constraining structures, play 'clever tricks' to score temporary 'victories of the weak over the strong' (De Certeau 1984: xix). The relevance of the notion of tactics becomes obvious when we consider that Gypsy-Travellers are invariably having to operate and survive on territory controlled by others. In such circumstances, the nomadic ideal and possibility of 'moving on', occupational flexibility coupled with a strong preference for self-employment and the absence of a clear work–leisure distinction all reveal 'tactical qualities': with space (largely) under the control of external powers, Travellers have indeed been observed (e.g. Okely 1983: 49–65) to 'manipulate time' –

through their alternative work routine that resists sedentary/ 'proletarianizing' control and, if nomadic, by deciding when to travel and how long to stay.

The nature of British Travellers' political mobilization since the 1960s also yields itself to a De Certeau-ian reading insofar as it reveals a preference for tactics over strategies (which would require a spatial power base or the quest for one). Tracing the organizational history of the Gypsy Council since its formation in a Kentish pub in 1966, Acton (1974) reveals the relatively limited appeal of Gypsy nationalism. Nationalism aims at 'making cultural and political units congruent' (Gellner 1983: 48), at making ethnic groups politically sovereign. Since it constitutes a territorial and institutional power base, the nation state is clearly defined by strategic characteristics. With some exceptions, Traveller calls for an independent state (of 'Romanestan') have been few and far between, nationalist ideas have been an 'inspiration to [only] a small group' of (British) Travellers but never a mass ideology (Acton 1974: 240). Most political mobilization has been aimed at the reform of existing state structures (to make them more accommodating to Travellers' ways of life), clearly favouring civil rights campaigns over movements concerned with the establishment of new institutions and power bases. 'Tactical' in character, most Travellers' resistance – patterned, collective and persistent though it may be – manifests itself mainly in time and practice rather than in a preoccupation with a specific space, the defended or fought-for power base that nationalism fetishizes.

In this section, we have briefly examined forms of symbolic group identification and everyday resistance as lived and articulated by some Travellers. Our discussion has drawn on Michel De Certeau's theoretical insights into the trickery of those who resist the tentacles and mechanisms of external power in their daily lives. In the process, we have complemented our earlier focus on processes of social classification and structural exclusion with an examination of culturally shared ideas and practices. Before returning to the tension between structural and cultural accounts of Traveller ethnicity mentioned above, we turn next to another key dimension to understanding ethnicity and everyday lives: power and resistance as also experienced *within* communities.

INTERNAL POWER AND RESISTANCE

In conceptualizing ethnicity as, in part, *structures of action* that enable and constrain – but do not fully determine – many of the everyday practices engaged in by members of an ethnic group, we also acknowledge the following crucial insight: not only is ethnicity significantly shaped by external power structures and cultural meaning (as we saw in the previous two sections), but social action *within* ethnic communities also implies role compliance (and/or 'deviance'), traditional expectations as to what constitutes 'acceptable' behaviour, decision-making mechanisms, inequalities of power, wealth and status; in other words, central to the notion of ethnic *structures of action* is the recognition that power also matters internally, that power is unequally distributed *within* ethnic communities along various axes including gender, age and class; such internal inequalities of power further imply the possibility of disagreement, contestation, conflict, resistance and cultural reinterpretations. In this section, we briefly examine some such internal inequalities among Gypsy-Travellers and provide a theoretical framework for them.

In the second volume of *The Practice of Everyday Life*, De Certeau and his colleague Luce Giard (1998: 254) argue that the contested territory of 'ordinary culture' is defined by two interrelated types of 'operations': first, an 'aesthetic' aspect, whereby 'everyday practice opens up a unique space within an imposed order'; and second, a 'polemical' aspect, which positions everyday practice in relation to the 'power relations that structure the social field'. This resonates with Traveller discourses and symbols of identity discussed above: the 'aesthetic' level captures cultural ideals of semi-nomadism and self-employment that are greatly valued, if not practised, by many Travellers (e.g. Okely 1983: 49–65, 128) as identity markers and hence celebrated as signs of ethnic uniqueness; at the same time, the 'polemical' aspect relates to the politics of their everyday lives, the lived ideological opposition to the sedentary system and its symbolic expression in some of the ideas and practices mentioned above. However, another crucial aspect to ethnicity and everyday life has so far been overlooked – the fact that the marginalized, excluded and resisting are, more often than not, internally structured and possibly conflict-ridden. In other words, how do class, gender, age, status and (relative) wealth shape the practices and life chances of different individuals *within* marginalized (ethnic) communities?

The literature on Travellers demonstrates that power, inequality, struggle and resistance do not stop at the external boundaries of caravan sites, but that they also define human relations within Traveller communities and families (i.e. across generations and between spouses). There is thus ample evidence of internal socio-economic status differences (e.g. Barnes 1975; Okely 1983), of inter-family feuds and lineage factionalism (e.g. Rehfisch and Rehfisch 1975; Barth 1975), of gendered power relations (e.g. Gmelch 1975), and of inter-generational conflicts over the value and desired extent of children's education (e.g. Kiddle 1999). Similarly, recent research on Romani communities in Central and Eastern Europe records patriarchal inequalities, social hierarchies and often deeply exploitative relations between different groups and families among the chronically excluded (e.g. Pogány 2004; Scheffel 2005).

In theoretical terms, this raises the question as to whether power and possible resistance need to be re-conceptualized in light of group divisions and internal conflicts. Contrary to the much-repeated criticism that Foucault overstates the effectiveness of power to the detriment of resistance (e.g. Belton 2005: 164), parts of his later work provide for these purposes a highly germane approach. In *The Will to Knowledge*, Foucault defines both power and resistance as multi-dimensional and ubiquitous, as encountered in every human relationship and potentially part of every encounter. His 'analytics' (Foucault 1998 [1976]: 98) includes several propositions suited to analysing group-internal (e.g. patriarchal and generational) inequalities alongside the wider power structures discussed above. Power, Foucault states, 'is everywhere'; 'exercised from numerous points' it constitutes a 'multiplicity of force relations'. Yet, 'where there is power there is resistance', more often than not 'mobile and transitory points of resistance, producing cleavages . . . [and] fracturing unities'. In other words, Foucault replaces the assumption that power is owned by the powerful and exercised on the powerless with a more nuanced account, which discovers both inequalities and struggle in multiple contexts and on every level of social reality.

Returning to Judith Okely's seminal ethnographic study, we encounter a telling example of the multi-dimensionality of both power and resistance that is worth quoting at length:

> There is a paradox embedded in the Gypsy women's role. [At home] she is hedged in by restrictions, expected to be subservient to her husband and cautious with other men. Yet nearly every day she [goes] out to 'enemy' territory [to] knock on doors of unknown people and establish contact with new customers. . . . There exist formal restrictions on the women's activities . . . [such as husbands] discouraging their wives from learning to drive [which] would give them considerable independence: 'I'm not having you running about, I want to know where you are.' . . . Nonetheless such controls . . . are . . . unenforceable. I discovered that women frequently conducted business with men alone and stressed the advantage.
>
> (Okely 1983: 205)

Patriarchal power and resistance to it here intersect with boundary maintenance between 'Gypsies' and 'Gorgios' in the context of everyday economic activities that inevitably bring the self into some contact with the other. Put another way, both micro- and macro-structures of power (i.e. within the family and across the ethnic boundary respectively) are being negotiated by Okely's female informants in their daily lives. This account of husbands' attempts to control their wives' activities and the women's 'micro-tactics of resistance' corroborate the Foucauldian definition of both power and resistance as multiple and omnipresent. As such, it also challenges any notion of ethnic communities as internally homogeneous or of ethnicity as the only factor circumscribing people's activities and life chances: *structures of action* are shaped by ethnic traditions as well as by patriarchal and other assumptions within them; however, they also involve the constant possibility of resistance.

This section has merely begun a discussion that will recur throughout this book concerning the multiple constraints on individuals exercised by cultural/religious traditions as well as by various structures of power and inequality (e.g. class, patriarchy). As we are beginning to see, however, personal idiosyncrasies and human agency exercise a strong influence on how these multiple constraints are variously endured, enacted, negotiated or contested. Before turning to the concluding section of this chapter, let me quote from a highly relevant account of a Hungarian Vlach Romani woman that summarizes these key themes:

> [C]ertainly every marriage has its own dynamic. Anikó, with her forceful personality and refusal to conform to the expectations of others, challenges many assumptions about . . . Vlach Romani women. . . . In many respects, Anikó is an emancipated Romani woman. . . . Traditionally, Romani women have been treated as 'second class' within Romani culture. However, broad generalisations have to be set against the sheer diversity of Romani practice . . . [and] subgroups. . . . Even within a particular Romani community, as Anikó has shown, strength of personality and other factors may go a long way to counteracting . . . cultural norms. For the most part, though, Romani women . . . live more circumscribed lives than their menfolk, often work much longer hours, enjoy less standing . . . and are expected to defer to men. Instances of domestic violence, in my experience at least, are depressingly common.
> (Pogány 2004: 115–116)

CONCLUSION

Thus we return to the two competing frameworks for understanding Traveller ethnicity mentioned at the beginning of this chapter: the culturalist and the structural approaches respectively, with the former emphasizing cultural and linguistic continuities traceable to northern India, while the latter holds that political mechanisms of classification, control and exclusion underlie the construction of 'the Gypsy other'. The discussion in this chapter has emphasized that there are significant truths in both approaches: drawing on Richard Jenkins (1997), I have argued that Gypsy-Traveller identities are the result of both external *social classification* (and concomitant processes of surveillance, control or exclusion) and internal *group identification* based on repertoires of culturally shared ideas, values and practices. In other words, both wider societal- and group-specific cultural factors have been shown to be implicated in the construction and reproduction of Traveller ethnicity. Travellers' everyday lives were thereby shown to be significantly shaped by external, often encroaching power and by ethnic *ways of seeing and acting* in the world premised on a notion of cultural difference and uniqueness. This was followed by a brief discussion of inequalities, power, resistance and conflict *within* Traveller communities.

All this said, an important question remains to be addressed concerning the representativeness of the cultural factors discussed above. All differences in interpretation notwithstanding, the contemporary literature is unanimous in stressing that the various categories of 'Romani', Traveller and 'Gypsy' contain vast internal diversities. István Pogány (2004: 75) thus refers to 'a common mistake, on part of the Gadje, to assume that Gypsies represent a single culture or people'; instead, he argues, 'identity among the Roma, is generally construed much more narrowly' and there is little sense of there being a unifying culture or history subsuming the many different, local communities with which people identify. Even Ian Hancock, a strong advocate of the culturalist approach, agrees that in light of intermarriage and historical change the notion of the 'pristine', 'true Romany' is now untenable (2002: 66). In other words, the effects of powerful outsiders on Gypsy-Travellers and the reality of vast cultural diversities among them emerge very clearly from the literature. The question thus arises how widespread are some of the cultural characteristics analysed by Judith Okely and discussed above. On one end of the spectrum, Hancock argues (2002: 68) that the binary division of the world into Romanies and non-Romanies, 'reinforced . . . by notions of cleanliness, eating habits, the handling of animals, sexual behaviour', is a defining characteristic of Romani communities everywhere. On the other end, some research suggests that there is 'hardly a trace' of notions of pollution and shame 'in the life styles or memory of increasing numbers of Roma in Central and Eastern Europe' (Pogány 2004: 22); conversely, Scheffel (2005: 97–98) observes that purity rules are being used among Slovak Roma as group-internal status markers, separating the local Romani elite from their chronically impoverished, 'underclass' co-ethnics. Taken together this strongly suggests that Okely's above-mentioned findings and analysis need to be contextualized – as evidence of certain cultural characteristics that were salient among particular Traveller communities at the time of her research and that resonate to a greater or lesser extent with similar ideas and practices among some Romani communities in other parts of the world. Historical context, local circumstances and group-specific appropriations (if any) will have a profound impact on the local form and prevalence (or otherwise) which such cultural characteristics will assume (see Bancroft 2005: 40).

Alongside her emphasis on cultural symbolisms of difference, Okely is also known for her scepticism concerning the 'single Indian origin thesis'. Other authors have taken issue with such scepticism: Angus Bancroft, for example, argues that 'questioning the assumed primordial origins of Gypsies or Travellers' can be tantamount to a 'discursive dismissal' of their identity and can thereby further disempower an already marginalized community of people; the problem, as Bancroft rightly points out (2005: 42–46), is that such arguments often leave the cultural and historical claims of powerful majorities intact and unquestioned: 'in the sense in which Gypsies can be said not to be an ethnic group, no community can be said to be an ethnic group, or for that matter a nation'. Seen in this light, debates about the respective impact of social processes of classification/exclusion and culture on Travellers' identities should be read as a general lesson about all ethnic identities. Concepts of genetic purity, cultural isolation and undiluted continuity are highly simplistic and dangerous figments of the political imagination; all discourses of ethnic belonging are symbolic constructs, though ones often powerfully grounded in (perceived or real) ancestry, shared memories and structures of inequality. The point is that the notion of a pure *ethnie* is rarely, if ever, sociologically tenable, yet it is an omnipresent and politically highly consequential part of everyday discourse. Romanies are no more and no less an ethnic group than any other thus designated; therefore, discounting their ethnicity is indeed potentially harmful and runs the risk of further silencing an already chronically marginalized community. All cultural histories are negotiated by individuals under conditions of unequally distributed power (and hence more or less strongly constrained choice). Romanies share this characteristic with all of us, though our respective positions in local, national and global webs of power are profoundly different. Consequently, all discourses of assumed 'belonging', all 'racial' and ethnic classifications should be subjected to critical scrutiny. Essentialist thought – the dangerous tendency to reduce complex individuals and groups to an assumed, singular, deep-seated cultural or racial 'format' – is as historically and sociologically untenable as it is politically motivated and harmful. Cultural change, multi-dimensional power structures and identities are omnipresent though frequently as well as conveniently overlooked social realities. In short, the complexities of Romani history teach us some universal lessons, which political actors intent upon forcing themselves and others into always unrealistically neat categories would be well advised to learn.

This is perfectly summarized by Brian Belton's autobiographical account and family history, which emphasize complex individuals at the expense of simplistic categories, and multiple sources of identification at the expense of rigid discourses of belonging. Belton's description of his 10-year-old son is worth quoting at length:

> [He] celebrates his East End, Gypsy, Gaelic, Flemish ancestry with a great deal of pride and humour, but . . . people know [him] simply as Christian, an eccentric, loving, sensitive, and intelligent little boy, a developing human being with a budding and interesting personality. He is intrigued by the world around him, his pet dog, Reg (a tubby and exuberant black Labrador), medieval history, the meaning of words, Warhammers, and the Simpsons. That is who he mostly and really is; *that* is *his* identity.
>
> (Belton 2005: 3)

Belton stresses the 'primacy of self' and the fact that we all negotiate the cultural traditions we are born into; this raises crucial issues of agency and the very concept of identity, to which we turn in the next chapter.

3

IDENTITY, DIASPORA, HYBRIDITY

The discussion presented in Chapter 2 concluded by emphasizing that (official) categories impinge significantly on, but do not fully determine, the groups which individuals recognize themselves as belonging to; *social classification* and *group identification* – the two dimensions explored thus far – provide highly significant constraints and parameters within which biographies and everyday lives are lived. As we shall discover in this chapter, however, systems of ethnic classification and cultural traditions do not tell the whole story. Continuing along the lines drawn by Brian Belton, we will explore the ways in which many individuals' life histories occur at the intersections of diverse cultural influences and are constrained by multiple power structures. Using sociological material on the so-called South Asian diaspora (with a focus on the UK), we will discover that individuals negotiate multiple *ways of seeing* the world and are subject to several *structures of action*; in light of relevant empirical material and theoretical insights, the very notion of an (ethnic) 'identity' will have to be rethought carefully and critically.

THEORIZING 'IDENTITY'

In an influential essay informed by a wide-ranging engagement with relevant social and cultural theory, Stuart Hall addresses the question as to how to conceptualize the notion of 'identity' particularly, though not exclusively, against the historical backdrop of our contemporary era. His starting point (1996: 2–4) is this: while identities are never stable or unified and 'in late modern times increasingly fragmented and fractured', to be able to confront some central sociological issues we none the less require a reformulated model of social identities or, more appropriately, identifications. In a nutshell, Hall's model partly resembles and crucially supplements Jenkins' distinction between *social classification* and *group identification* as two interrelated processes constitutive of (ethnic) identities. To Stuart Hall power structures are indeed crucial – through their institutional and linguistic/discursive practices – in creating certain positions and allocating or 'attaching' people to them. At the same time, however, a process of identification – on the part of the people addressed by power/discourse – with such 'subject positions' is also a prerequisite for identities to be 'achieved':

> I use 'identity' to refer to the meeting point, the point of suture between on the one hand the discourses and practices which attempt to 'interpellate', speak to us or hail us into place as the social subjects of particular discourses, and on the other hand, the processes which produce subjectivities, which construct us as subjects which can be 'spoken'. Identities are thus points of temporary attachment to the subject positions which discursive practices construct for us. . . . They are the result of a successful articulation or 'chaining' of the subject into the flow of the discourse.
>
> (Hall 1996: 5–6)

Projecting this on to our conceptual framework of ethnicity, *ways of seeing* the world and *structures of action* thus emerge as discourses, practices and institutions that speak to people, and attempt to define them and their place in the world. Individuals' acceptance of, and compliance with, the frameworks of interpretation and expected behaviours and roles 'provided' by cultural traditions form the second definitional requirement for an ethnic identity to come about. Hall's model advances the discussion of (ethnic) identities in two crucial respects. First, he moves the analytical focus from the group to the individual: the effective articulation of an identity requires subjects to 'invest in the position' (1996: 6) allocated to them. In other words, identities implicate two core dimensions – the individual's psyche and the power structures that surround and impinge on them. Second, at the heart of Hall's model is his insistence that individuals' attachment to a subject position, their successful 'summoning into place', is only ever achieved temporarily:

> [T]he discursive approach sees identification as a construction, a process never completed – always 'in process'. It is not determined in the sense that it can . . . be 'won' or 'lost', sustained or abandoned. Though not without its determinate conditions of existence, including the material and symbolic resources required to sustain it, identification is in the end conditional, lodged in contingency.
>
> (Hall 1996: 2–3)

Such contingency thus creates 'subjects-in-process', whose identities – Hall argues – draw on 'the resources of history, language and culture in the process of becoming rather than being'; multiply constrained by, and positioned within, various structures of power and inequality, subjects possess and exhibit (some) agency in their uses and negotiations of the discourses that aim to define them and the (cultural) practices that involve them (also see Knowles 1999). Hall famously declares that identities are 'constituted within, not outside representation . . . [they are] not the so-called return to roots, but a coming-to-terms-with our "routes"' (1996: 4).

This chapter demonstrates the relevance of Hall's model for an analysis of contemporary South Asian identities in the UK. Before turning to a further and complementary theoretical perspective, the following summary of Hall's key themes – discursive practices as the linguistic manifestation of power, the 'symbolic resources' provided by history and culture, the subject and their creative capacity for negotiation and resistance – is worth quoting at length:

> The question which remains is . . . what the mechanisms are by which individuals identify (or do not identify) with the 'positions' to which they are summoned; as well as how they fashion, stylize, produce and 'perform' these positions, and why they never do so completely, for once and all time, and some never do, or are in a constant . . . process of struggling with, resisting, negotiating and accommodating the

normative or regulative rules with which they confront and regulate themselves.

(Hall 1996: 13–14)

In very general terms, Stuart Hall here provides some profound insights concerning the complexity of social identities, the relationships between individuals and the contexts they are born and socialized into, the structural positions and cultural histories that significantly shape – without being able to fully determine – social actors' biographies. Read more narrowly, in asking these questions Hall also teaches us some of the most important lessons pertaining to ethnicity and everyday life: the *ways of seeing* and *structures of action* furnished by the former are being *negotiated* in the realm of the latter. In other words, ethnicity provides frameworks of understanding the world and social networks of both support and obligation; by virtue of their membership in such a network, individuals are expected to subscribe to its accounts of the world (and the group's place within it) and also to fulfil cultural expectations of internal solidarity and role compliance. However, (everyday) life is far more complex than this – people reinterpret and possibly challenge traditional ways of understanding the world and oppose entrenched ways of acting in it. Human agency is thus a key reason for why the 'fit' between a culturally defined subject position and our actual identities – as lived and hence open to (some) negotiation – is an imperfect and indeterminate one.

There are, as we shall see, other related and hugely important factors that affect individuals' negotiations of the subject positions widely assumed to constitute 'their identities'. Most crucially, individuals are subject to multiple power structures and their corresponding discursive practices. This has been comprehensively analysed by Avtar Brah (1996), who speaks of the intersection (or 'articulation') of multiple 'axes of power, inequality, and exclusion', including class, gender, race, ethnicity, nationality and sexuality. 'Subject positions' are 'provided' on each of these axes, or – more accurately – individuals are, often more or less simultaneously, 'hailed' into different places along these different axes. Not only are identities not unitary, neither is power; lives are profoundly shaped by different and co-existing systems of exclusion, which intersect in multiple and complex ways: 'structures of class, racism, gender and sexuality cannot be treated as "independent variables" because the oppression of each is inscribed within the other' (Brah 1996: 109). Identities are thus perpetually being negotiated in relation to such multi-dimensional struggles and inequalities. To provide a hypothetical example, we may ponder what 'identity' might mean for a sub-Saharan asylum seeker who is also a single mother; or perhaps for a working-class Muslim; or for a homosexual member of a conservative, evangelical Christian congregation. In each of these cases and yet in ways that are particular to each, 'identities' are indeed multi-dimensional and profoundly shaped by several systems of inequality and exclusion; and, continuing with Stuart Hall, we would surely have to conclude that such broad descriptive labels tell us very little, if anything, about how specific individuals negotiate their several 'positions' in an unequal world and as part of their everyday lives.

Moreover, people inhabit – particularly but by no means exclusively in 'late modern' times – social spaces in which different cultural traditions intersect, overlap, shape one another, are merged into new, emerging, so-called hybrid identities. In other words, different *ways of seeing*, *structures of action and feeling* associated with distinct ethnicities 'meet' in the biographies and everyday lives of social actors who cannot be confined or reduced to any one 'culture' without their complexity – we might say their humanity – being seriously distorted. This is not, of course, to argue that people choose freely from a range of ethnic traditions on offer: different *structures of action* impinge on them in different contexts and, depending on biographical circumstances, to different degrees; negotiation – and hence agency – is always constrained, to a greater or lesser extent, by the power structures to which individuals are subject. However, the point is that 'cultures' do not constitute self-contained universes that fully determine who an individual is, what they do and think. Instead, social actors exhibit some (more or less) constrained choice as to how they manoeuvre amidst culturally heterogeneous traditions, pushes and pulls.

SOUTH ASIAN AND BRITISH

The much-quoted fourth national survey of ethnic minorities in Britain (Modood *et al.* 1997), carried out in 1994 with a representative sample of people of Caribbean and Asian origin (and a white comparison group), reveals a complex picture that includes several core findings (Berthoud *et al.* 1997: 1–10). First, it shows that structural disadvantages, racial exclusion and inequality continue but 'do not operate uniformly' across all ethnic minority groups; considerable upward social mobility by some groups thus sits juxtaposed to the continuing marginalization suffered by others. Second, very significant diversity of origin, socio-economic position and 'life style' is not only found between people of Caribbean and Asian origin but, crucially, also *within* these demographic categories. Third, the survey reveals the complexity of self-definitions – the increasingly widespread identification with Britain on one end of the spectrum, and 'ethnic assertiveness, arising out of the feelings of not being respected or of lacking access to public space' (Berthoud *et al.* 1997: 7), on the other.

In the categories of the 2001 census, there are more than 2.2 million people of South Asian descent living in the UK, more than a million of whom are of Indian, more than 700,000 of Pakistani, and nearly 300,000 of Bangladeshi background (Hussain 2005: 19). Building on the theoretical strands presented in the previous section, we now turn to the question as to what '(ethnic) identity' might mean to some British South Asians. To do so, we will examine recent sociological and anthropological analyses of both the structural positions and the complex cultural dynamics in specific localities inhabited, in part, by members of the South Asian diaspora. Diaspora constitutes a nowadays much-used term, which – along with the notions of hybridity and syncretism – will require some debate and conceptual clarification. To begin with, however, we need to provide a brief summary of the history of South Asian migration and settlement in the UK, and of some of the social characteristics encountered among groups variously identified as Indian, Pakistani and Bangladeshi.

History and diversity

While 'adventurers' and small communities of seamen had settled in Britain over the previous two centuries or more, mass migration from South Asia to the UK did not start until after World War II. In the context of the 'post-war boom' and acute labour shortages in the British industrial economy between the early 1950s and the 1970s, 'migrant workers [were] drawn from . . . the islands of the Caribbean and from the Indian subcontinent' (Ballard 1994a: 5–6). Many South Asian workers initially intended for their stays to be temporary and a means of socio-economic mobility – through higher wages and remittances – for themselves and their extended families at home. However, the so-called 'myth of return' soon gave way to permanent settlement. Family reunions, starting in the 1960s, were a major factor in this process, which was influenced by increasingly restrictive immigration and employment legislation but also constituted a way of 'preserving and protecting' the networks and reciprocities of kinship (Shaw 1994). Most of the early migrants originated from the rural Punjab (both its western Pakistani and eastern Indian parts), the state of Gujarat in north-western India and from the Sylhet district of what is now Bangladesh. A second period of South Asian migration to the UK, during the late 1960s and the early 1970s, involved the descendants of Punjabi indentured labourers and, in particular, of Gujarati craftsmen and traders who had migrated to East Africa (e.g. Kenya, Uganda) during the nineteenth and early twentieth centuries (e.g. Dwyer 1994). Following decolonization, many East African Asians became the target of racial persecution, which climaxed most infamously in their mass expulsion from Uganda at the hands of Idi Amin in 1972. Their unwanted exodus from East Africa transformed them – often after periods of intense fear, economic dispossession as well as bureaucratic uncertainty – into 'twice migrants', and took many as Commonwealth citizens (and despite increasingly restrictive immigration legislation) to the UK (e.g. Warrier 1994; Bloch 2002: 35).

Such diverse trajectories and histories of migration to Britain showed two important common denominators: first, experiences of racial hostility and often marginalization upon settlement; second, both the 'first generation' of settlers and their British-born offspring have found 'inspiration in the resources of their own particular cultural, religious and linguistic inheritance, which they are . . . creatively reinterpreting in order to rebuild their lives' (Ballard 1994a: 5). In the wider conceptual terms guiding our discussion, this again highlights two crucial aspects to understanding ethnicity and everyday life: on the one hand, the centrality of (wider) relations of power and exclusion, which impose constraints on people's life chances and conditions; and, on the other, the instrumentalist observation that ethnicity can provide a much-needed network of support and culturally shared meaning in conditions of struggle and adversity.

As indicated above, the very broad category 'British South Asian' subsumes a tremendous 'plurality of identities' (Hussain 2005: 132). This internal diversity cannot be reduced to the only slightly more nuanced labels 'Indian', 'Pakistani' and 'Bangladeshi' either, but requires the multi-dimensional and processual conceptualization of power and identities provided above. The several 'axes of differentiation' (Brah 1996), in relation to which South Asian everyday lives are lived and identities negotiated, include the following: regional (and linguistic) background, religious (and sectarian) affiliation, class, gender, caste, and history of migration. Crucially, these multiple dimensions of power and difference do indeed cross-cut one another in complex ways and are also, as we shall see, variously and inevitably affected by both the 'diasporic experience' and the wider historical parameters provided by our contemporary era.

The various regional backgrounds of both the early and twice migrants and the transnational significance of kinship obligations have already been mentioned. It must be further noted that networks of extended kin were a major factor facilitating (particularly in the early years) 'chain migration', as a result of which 'specific and highly localised . . . kinship groups have given rise to – and are now umbilically linked with – equally tightly structured British based ethnic colonies' (Ballard 1994a: 11). In other words, not only regions of origin but far more specific localities and social relationships within those significantly shaped patterns of migration and settlement. The complex intersection of regional and religious backgrounds becomes apparent when we consider that, while the majority of Pakistani Punjabis are Muslims and the majority of Indian Punjabis Sikhs, they contain small Christian and significant Hindu 'minorities' respectively; and while the majority of Gujarati migrants are Hindus, there is also a sizeable Muslim community among them; Sylheti Bangladeshis are overwhelmingly Muslims; there are also smaller diasporic groups of Zoroastrian Parsis, Jains, Buddhists and South Asian Christians (Ballard 1994a: 20–21). Moreover (and contrary to popular stereotypes), particularly the broad religious categories of Hindu (e.g. Dwyer 1994), South Asian Muslim (e.g. Lewis 1994) and Sikh (e.g. Ballard 1994b) are internally highly differentiated along sectarian lines, devotional preference, or affiliation to various contemporary movements of religious reform and political mobilization.

The South Asian diaspora has also been profoundly shaped by, and continues to be internally differentiated along, class lines – by economically structured inequalities that are grounded in people's relative position in existing relations of production and that manifest themselves not only materially but also symbolically (e.g. Anthias 2001; Sayer 2002). Indeed, the effects of class (i.e. difference and exclusion) have impacted on every stage of migration and settlement. In the first instance, migrants are usually from families of 'middling status, whose members are neither sufficiently prosperous to be wholly content . . . nor so poor as to be unable to afford the migrant's ticket, passport and visa' (Ballard 1994a: 10). That said, Bangladeshi migrants were, in general, from considerably poorer backgrounds than were Punjabis and Gujaratis, a profound socio-economic disadvantage that affects large sections of the Bangladeshi diaspora to this day (see below). Subsequently, many South Asian migrants/settlers and their families bore the brunt of economic 'restructuring' during the 1980s, when demand for unskilled industrial labour declined rapidly (Ballard 1994a: 6). As we shall see in due course, a history of structural disadvantage (e.g. in the areas of employment and, particularly in the early years, housing) forms a key part to any understanding of British South Asian identities. On the opposite end of the (class) spectrum, Gujarati migrants, many of them twice migrants who endured and escaped racial persecution in East Africa, are among the most upwardly mobile, 'affluent and successful of Britain's South Asian settlers' (Dwyer 1994: 165).

A further and, in South Asian contexts, highly consequential source of differential power and inequality is provided by caste: this is a traditional, steeply hierarchical system of occupational and ritual specialization, embedded in Hindu cosmology and based on endogamous groups with inherited status. While caste hierarchies have of course been profoundly affected by the far-reaching social changes of modernity, related ideas and practices – as manifest in religious rituals, strong preferences for marriage within one's caste, and notions of purity and pollution – continue to matter greatly. Moreover, caste differences have also been transplanted into parts of the diaspora, where they underpin continuing preferences for caste endogamy and certain forms of social mobilization (i.e. caste associations). However, as pointed out by Brah (1996: 30), 'caste in Britain is not an exact replica of caste in India; rather, British-based configurations of caste have their own specific features'. Moreover, even though both Islam and Sikhism oppose – on a doctrinal level – the Hindu concept of caste, widespread ideas of ritual (im-)purity, endogamous marriage patterns and the (in rural contexts) still common hereditary ascription of occupational status suggest that 'few if any of the subcontinent's non-Hindu communities have remained immune from [the] influence' of caste (Ballard 1994a: 27).

Much of our subsequent discussion will centre on gender and its intersection with some of these wider and group-internal power structures. Suffice it for now to mention that family reunion and the transformation of migrant workers into permanent settlers also heightened the cultural significance of personal and family honour discourses (*izzat*) in many British South Asian communities. Such discourses are not only gendered but also a means of cultural boundary maintenance and an instance of ethnicity providing both *ways of seeing* the world and *structures of action*. As we shall see, however, everyday life also crucially involves cultural change, human agency, as well as multi-dimensional identities and strategies for living in a world of multiple inequalities.

Diaspora

Debates about British South Asian identities tend to draw on the notion of 'diaspora', which conventionally refers to the transnational dispersal of a cultural community. Thus defined as 'a particular type of ethnic category . . . that exists across the boundaries of nation states rather than within them', certain conceptualizations of 'diaspora' have been criticized for reinforcing primordial and hence 'absolutist notions of "origin" and "true belonging"'(Anthias 1998: 571, 577). This must serve as a crucial word of warning for us not to become complicit with political mechanisms of exclusion and marginalization that define communities of migrants and settlers as the irrevocable 'other', allegedly grounded in a distant homeland and hence fundamentally different from 'us'. However, there are significant contributions to the literature on diaspora that clearly oppose such political populism while providing important conceptual insights into the everyday lives of countless millions of people, both 'settlers' and their neighbours who may think of themselves as 'indigenous'.

One such contribution emerges from Marie Gillespie's ethnographic study of patterns of media consumption and cultural change among Punjabi youths in the London suburb of Southall. Gillespie's analysis is based on an appreciation of the multiple, transnational social relationships that define the lives of her informants:

> A diasporic perspective situates Punjabi families in relation to the web of connections between Punjabis in the Indian subcontinent, in various parts of Britain (Southall, Birmingham and Leeds being the main centres of settlement), in Germany, Canada and the USA. Many in Southall are also 'twice migrants', having formerly lived in East Africa.
>
> (Gillespie 1995: 6)

Steven Vertovec (2000: 147) supplements such a perspective by distinguishing between 'three meanings of diaspora': first (and corroborating Gillespie's account of a multi-dimensional 'web of connections'), Vertovec argues that diasporas entail 'triadic' social relationships between a current place of residence, the original or perceived homeland, and other nodes or locations in the transnational ethnic network; second, Vertovec defines diasporas as a 'type of consciousness' or 'state of mind' informed by an 'awareness of multi-locality'; and, third, diaspora encompasses forms of 'cultural production and reproduction' aided, in part, by modern communication technologies. In the following discussion we encounter some of the empirical evidence indicating that British South Asian identities do indeed incorporate these three dimensions of diaspora: transnational social relationships (and corresponding economic/political strategies of mobilization, cultural reproduction and potential social mobility); a type of consciousness that is simultaneously global and local; and contemporary forms of cultural activity (or signifying practices), through which (ethnic) identities are being articulated and negotiated.

Vertovec makes a further highly relevant contribution to discussions of diaspora and the relationship between culture and ethnicity: he suggests (2000: 64) that migration and settlement (frequently defined by experiences of hostility, discrimination and racial exclusionism) provide conditions conducive to the transformation of the Bourdieu-ian *habitus* – taken-for-granted and culturally shared dispositions, tastes, categories and everyday practices – into 'ethnic ideologies' that can become the rationale for political mobilization. As discussed in Chapter 1, this presents not only a compelling framework for thinking about the relationship between commonsensical culture and self-consciously articulated ethnic identities, but also a plausible account of high levels of political activism observed among many diaspora communities. Put another way, this suggests that migrants' frequent participation in both local and so-called 'homeland politics' may be linked to the consciousness-raising effects of dislocation and discrimination, that the common experience of crises can trigger reflection and identity politics. More fundamentally, in emphasizing wider relations of inequality and exclusion, Vertovec reminds us that understanding diasporas requires a close look at power.

In this context, we must once again return to Avtar Brah, whose 'multi-axial understanding of power' has already been summarized as one of our main sources of theoretical guidance. In *Cartographies of Diaspora* Brah applies this conceptualization of power to make three further arguments that are of central relevance to our discussion in this chapter. First, she emphasizes that the intersection of various axes of inequality and exclusion including gender, class, 'race', ethnicity and sexuality gives rise to 'configurations of power which differentiate diasporas internally' as well as in relation to their wider social fields (1996: 183); this, of course, provides theoretical corroboration for our earlier summary of the complex interactions of class, gender, religion, caste and migratory histories in the biographies of South Asian migrants and their descendants. Second, Brah emphasizes the possibility of 'resistance to the processes of exclusion' (1996: 176), thus reminding us that identities implicate both external power structures and subjectivities with the potential for (some) subversion and contestation. Third (and, as we shall see, crucially), Brah moves the discussion from a narrow focus on the 'migrant other' to the more encompassing idea of 'diaspora space':

> My argument is that diaspora space . . . is 'inhabited', not only by those who have migrated and their descendants, but equally by those who are constructed and represented as indigenous. In other words, the concept of *diaspora space* (as opposed to diaspora) includes the . . . intertwining of the genealogies of dispersion with those of 'staying put'.
>
> (Brah 1996: 209)

Of course, Brah emphasizes that migration and 'staying put' involve vastly different subject positions in the 'complex web of power' that places and constrains individuals and groups. However, in speaking of such 'diaspora space' Brah avoids the above-mentioned dangers of migrants being constructed and excluded as the 'primordial other'. Instead, the concept of 'diaspora space' implicates all of us, it captures ethnic diversity as a hallmark of our time, while grounding its analysis in an appreciation of the complex effects of multi-dimensional inequalities and the possibility of resistance through critical consciousness. In other words, Brah's concept of diaspora space also connects with our earlier framework for thinking about the everyday based on the parameters of historical context, power/resistance and reflexivity (or lack thereof).

EVERYDAY IDENTITIES: MARGINALIZATION, GENDER, RELIGION AND CHANGE

The crux of the argument presented in this chapter thus far has been twofold. First, we have examined relevant theories (e.g. Hall 1996) that conceptualize identity as an ongoing process involving multiple structures of power and the individuals who are subject to them, yet who are able, to a greater or lesser extent, to negotiate and potentially contest their 'subject positions' (and corresponding expected behaviours). Second, our summary of the history of South Asian migration and diaspora presence in the UK has revealed a great deal of internal heterogeneity as well as cross-cutting loyalties and divisions. One obvious question that follows from this is how, in the face of such internal diversity, the concept of an overarching 'Asian identity' came about and if, as well as why, individual social actors came to recognize and 'invest in' it. Following a brief discussion of this question, we will examine existing evidence of several, often uneasily co-existing discourses of identity, in relation to which actual identifications are negotiated, exclusions endured and meaningful lives maintained.

Emerging 'Asian' identities

Turning once more to Avtar Brah, we discover how social classification – as a function of power – impacts on generation-specific everyday lives and hence on historically changing subjectivities. More accurately, Brah demonstrates how in Britain between the 1950s and 1980s '"the Asian" was constructed in different discourses, policies, and practices ... and how these constructions were appropriated or contested by the political agency of Asian subjects' (1996: 17). Tracing the contemporary South Asian presence in the UK through its different trajectories of migration to its various regional and social origins, Brah isolates a number of common denominators and experiences: the overwhelming majority of the early migrants found themselves occupying the bottom end of the socio-economic hierarchy, working extremely long hours in unskilled employment, and living in poor housing; many migrants experienced racial hostility and sometimes violence; important decisions, such as family reunions, were significantly shaped by increasingly restrictive immigration legislation; the latter was partly indicative of a changing focus, in dominant discourses, away from the problems faced by immigrants to immigrants themselves being seen as 'constituting "a problem"' (Brah 1996: 27). Even more crucial perhaps was the 'coming of age' of a British-born and increasingly self-assertive generation:

> The emergence of the youth groups marks . . . a new form of Asian political and cultural agency. . . . [H]aving grown up in Britain, they articulate a *home-grown British political discourse*. They lay claim to the localities in which they live as their 'home'. And, however much they may be constructed as 'outsiders', they contest these psychological and geographical spaces from the position of 'insiders'. Even when they describe themselves as 'Asian', this is not a reaching back to some 'primordial Asian' identity. What they are speaking of is a modality of 'British Asian-ness'.
>
> (Brah 1996: 47; emphasis in original)

In the context of external mechanisms of classification and exclusion but also significantly thanks to their own political activism and symbolic creativity, the so-called 'second generation' – the sons and daughters of the initial migrants/settlers – 'acquired' an additional subject position: the newly constructed category of 'British Asian-ness', based on an assertion of *both* Britishness *and* ethnic distinctiveness, now sits alongside – albeit not always comfortably – other sources of identification 'inherited' by virtue of an individual's gender, their ethnic, religious, caste, and class backgrounds. Moreover, since the 1980s British Asian-ness has also found symbolic expression through various forms of cultural production. These include the hugely popular reappropriation of *bhangra*, originally a folk dance from the rural Punjab, which in its creative, diasporic re-invention has come to be 'embraced by young British Asians of every ethnic origin' (Gillespie 1995: 45). Gerd Baumann's ethnography of the above-mentioned London suburb of Southall confirms the significance of cultural signifying practices such as *bhangra* to 'young Southallians' conceptualization of a new *Asian culture*': this is generation-specific, given that their parents often continue to define themselves with reference to religious membership (i.e. Sikh, Hindu, Muslim), to regional/national (i.e. Punjabi, Gujarati, Bangladeshi) or more narrowly defined local origins; even for the young generation, however, it must be noted that 'British Asian-ness' has not displaced these older sources of self-definition and culturally shared meaning;

instead, the articulation of British Asian-ness should be understood as an example of solidarities and identities being partly re-negotiated, of cultural practices and traditions being contextually and imaginatively reappropriated:

> [Young Southallians] tend, by an overwhelming majority, to marry within their own *communities* of religion, as well as caste; those who do not, tend to leave Southall. Yet the discovery of an *Asian culture* and *community* among the young presents a first example of the processes by which *culture* and *community* become objects of debate and terms of contestation.
>
> (Baumann 1996: 157; emphasis in original)

Ethnic *structures of action*, here reflected in the rules of religious/ caste endogamy, persist (as do the social boundaries thus delineated); and yet cultural meanings and identities are subject to historical change as alternative identities become available – in particular circumstances and in addition to established ones. What we are beginning to observe, then, is clearly not an unconstrained form of agency but social actors who are culturally embedded, structurally positioned, and who strive for recognition, fulfilment and meaningful lives. They do so by negotiating their several subject positions in existing configurations of power and inequality, by mobilizing and – if possible, considered useful, interesting or exciting – by engaging creatively with the cultural resources at their disposal.

All this being said, the subject position provided by 'British Asian-ness' is in turn internally contested, not least by discourses of religious belonging and revival. This raises further significant questions: within the constrained choice available to them, what attracts individuals to a particular subject position rather than existing alternatives? What makes a discourse of Hindu, Sikh, or Islamic solidarity more appealing to some young people than the alternative, more encompassing notion of British Asian-ness? Let me stress that these are highly complex issues that I can merely hope to raise but do not purport to answer. However, whatever a possible answer might be, it would clearly need to account for important structural factors.

Socio-economics

To state that everyday lives are crucially shaped by employment patterns and income levels is to make an obvious yet crucial point. I have already mentioned that the 1994 national survey of ethnic minorities (Modood *et al.* 1997) revealed very considerable socio-economic diversity *within* the 'British South Asian' category. Subjecting the same source of data to further statistical analysis, Mark Brown (2000) has examined the very diverse economic experiences of different British South Asian communities as manifest in the three areas of proportion of 'working age population' in paid employment, employment type of those in work and differences in income. Brown's findings confirm that economic activity and experiences of discrimination in the labour market vary very significantly along religious lines but also, and crucially, with areas of origin. Thus, while unemployment levels were particularly high and average incomes considerably lower among Muslims than other religious groupings, the picture is complicated by the fact that Indian Muslims were economically more secure and considerably more affluent than Pakistanis and Bangladeshis; Hindus showed the highest proportions of young people in full-time education, of full-time employment, and – importantly along with Indian Muslims – of people employed in high-status, high-earning managerial or professional jobs; conversely, Sikhs were more likely to be unemployed and/or to be dependent on self-employment, as a 'strategy in dealing with structural unemployment and a discriminatory labour market' (Brown 2000: 1054), than Hindus. The intersection of ethnicity, religion and gender was revealed by the fact that, in general, the proportion of women in managerial/ professional occupations was very considerably lower and differences by religious background less pronounced, strongly suggesting that patriarchy cross-cuts religious divisions. The complex interactions of ethnicity and class emerged from the finding that 'semi-skilled and unskilled jobs account for one quarter and 40 per cent respectively of Sikhs and Pakistani/Bangladeshi Muslims, compared to less than one in five of other groups'; moreover, semi- and unskilled workers were far more likely to be unemployed than those near the top of the occupational hierarchy, a painful fact reflected in 'the massive rise in

Pakistani unemployment following collapse of the textile industry' in the 1980s (Brown 2000: 1048, 1059).

The over-representation of Pakistanis and Bangladeshis among the economically marginalized and vulnerable is often seen as evidence of widespread Islamophobic prejudice and discrimination. That said, the contrasting positions of relative advantage occupied by a significant proportion of Indian Muslims suggest that migrants' and settlers' life chances are shaped not only by structures of exclusion encountered in the diaspora. Other consequential factors include the histories, circumstances and trajectories of migration, regions of origin and their often very different economic and educational structures, local cultural traditions and 'differences in human capital' (Brown 2000: 1058) 'inherited', to a greater or lesser extent, by the 'second generation'. Hasmita Ramji's more localized study of the intersections of class, ethnicity, gender, religion and identity politics among British Pakistani men in Blackburn illuminates some of this complexity. Ramji starts by citing some extremely disconcerting statistics that report unemployment levels among British Pakistani male youth as up to five times of those among their white counterparts. Moreover, 'they are most likely to get the worst jobs, the lowest wage and face widespread discrimination. Even after allowances for education and residential area, Pakistani Muslims are three times more likely to be jobless than Indian Hindus are' (Ramji 2005: 3.1). Clearly and rightly sceptical of generalizations and simplistic 'explanations' (also see Dench et al. 2006), Ramji reports her interview findings that reflect heterogeneous experiences among the Pakistani community of Blackburn: her sample included young men in semi- or unskilled (as well as often temporary and uncertain) employment as well as young professionals; not only did the two groups occupy very different structural positions, but they also articulated vastly different identity discourses. The former saw their 'underclass position' as closely related to their ethnic identities; class and racial exclusionism were seen as closely intertwined. In this context, they articulated a strong sense of collective identity – one informed by their status as British Pakistanis as well as, crucially, by Islam: while the former was experienced as a subject position of economic disadvantage and permanent marginalization, a discourse of Islamic identity provided a boundary marker both *vis-à-vis* the white majority and in relation to their parental generation; the latter, some of Ramji's interviewees argued, did not understand Islam 'properly' and had wrongly conflated their traditional, localized cultures with 'real Islam'. By contrast, Ramji's sample of British Pakistani middle-class professionals articulated a discourse of identity that was informed by a meritocratic view of social mobility, was centred on the individual, de-emphasized the significance of religion (and actively opposed pan-Islamic ideologies), and insisted on the compatibility of Pakistani ethnicity with cosmopolitan, British, middle-class 'spaces' (Ramji 2005: 6.9).

At this point it should be noted that while ideologies and movements of Islamic revivalism need to be understood in their wider contexts of socio-economic marginalization (e.g. Berthoud *et al*. 1997: 9), exclusive discourses of religious belonging are neither peculiar to Islam nor to the economically most disenfranchised. Comparable rejections of the pan-ethnic/trans-religious discourse of British Asian-ness have also been observed among (relatively privileged) Hindu university students against the backdrop of the rise of Hindu nationalism in the 1990s (Raj 2000), and among parts of the Sikh diaspora in the context of the transnational movement for an independent (state of) Khalistan in the Punjab a decade earlier (e.g. Kinnvall 2002). All this being said, and lest the impression be conveyed that identities are fixed and static after all, we now turn to evidence corroborating their multi-faceted and historically changing character.

Changing traditions and the everyday

Some of the studies cited in the previous section seemingly support the suggestion that a recent 'shift in identification from culture to religion has created a further [internal] barrier' (Hussain 2005: 19), thus eroding the fragile construct of British Asian-ness from within. However, there are several reasons why such a conclusion would be premature. Most importantly, ideologies of exclusive religious belonging are – in Stuart Hall's terminology – only among numerous competing discourses of identity articulated to 'attach' individuals to the 'subject positions' they construct. Ethnic or religious *ways of seeing* and *structures of action* can variously constrain individuals and make their lives meaningful; in either case, they do not hold a monopoly of power over the people they 'interpellate' (or speak to). It is undoubtedly the case in our contemporary era that increasing numbers of people identify with, and 'invest in', the narrowly defined subject positions provided by sometimes externally hostile discourses of (religious) belonging. As we are beginning to see, however, everyday lives and biographies are constrained by multiple power structures and their discursive practices. The challenge, then, is to account for individuals' constrained choice of one discourse over another, made in particular contexts and to the backdrop of the ongoing processes of their identity negotiations. Moreover, such processes do not only involve ideologies that have caught politicians' and the media's attention in recent years. Identity negotiations and cultural change also occur in far more banal ways, in the everyday lives of so-called 'ordinary people'.

This is powerfully demonstrated in Surinder Guru's study (2003) of six families comprising three generations of mothers and daughters, of (Sikh) Punjabi origin (and of different caste and class backgrounds), living in Britain. Guru's research addresses several of our key themes including the intersections of religion, ethnicity, caste, class and gender. More generally, she demonstrates that everyday life is a deeply political realm in which individuals negotiate and reinterpret cultural traditions and expectations. As a result, ethnic *ways of seeing* the world and existing *structures of action* are shown to be subject to historical, inter-generational change. Guru's starting point is that despite Sikhism's religious message of equality, women's lives are constrained by gendered (and caste-like) inequalities manifest in rules of endogamy and the above-mentioned code of family honour (*izzat*). The latter is deeply gendered, defining Punjabi femininity in terms of 'submission, modesty, sexual purity, domestication and obedience as virtues of womanhood', and is reflected in cultural expectations concerning women's dress, language, food consumption and public demeanour (Guru 2003: 5–8). Part of the cultural *habitus*, such perceptions of 'ideal' femininity are imbued throughout socialization and play a crucial part in the reproduction of patriarchal family structures. As Guru also points out, however, there is considerable variation between orthodox, liberal and radical families as to how such rules, notions and structures are variously appropriated or resisted. Moreover, Guru's interview findings show that while the first generation of women settlers tended to be fairly conservative in accepting established notions of *izzat*, the second generation started a process of often conflict-laden cultural reinterpretation. Conscious of the effects of racism and also aware of the feminist critique, some second-generation British Punjabi women challenged inequalities endured both by ethnic minorities and within them. That said, their ability to do so depended 'as much on their material resources and support networks as on their emotional and psychological strength to confront oppressive practices' (Guru 2003: 10). One of Guru's informants provides revealing insights into human agency, cultural change and the possible costs of challenging established *structures of action*:

> Ranjeet ... met her future husband and when her parents refused permission for her marriage, primarily because of his lower caste, she left home and lost communication with them for ten years. Having been ostracized by ... the wider family networks, she married of her own accord and continued with her studies to acquire professional qualifications leading to a well-paid, secure, high-status employment and then rebuilt her relationship with her natal family. In the process she now considered herself ... a feminist and had chosen what to take on from her Asian upbringing: 'I think I've put the culture through a sieve and I've got the bits that I like and abandoned the bits I don't like.'
>
> (Guru 2003: 12–13)

Such biographies provide clear evidence of individuals actively negotiating their cultural heritage and of everyday life constituting a key site for their potential resistance to the subject positions they are expected to assume. While such negotiations and struggles can certainly redefine cultural meanings and reconfigure power relations, changes are likely to be piecemeal (and in turn contested) rather than definitive or complete. This emerges from Guru's observation that these second-generation British Punjabi women still articulate strong preferences for endogamy, though defined in wider religious/national terms (rather than in terms of caste, as their parents did), as they bring up their own daughters. Ranjeet is thus also quoted as saying that while she 'wouldn't condone a relationship with a Muslim or Afro-Caribbean' she would ultimately, in such a case, have to 'go along with it' (Guru 2003: 17).

Not only are complex, multi-faceted British Asian identities experienced in relation to important life decisions, but they are also continually – and hence in the course of everyday life – being negotiated in the consumption of both local and global news media. This is illuminated in Marie Gillespie's above-mentioned study of *Television, Ethnicity and Cultural Change* (1995) based on long-term ethnographic fieldwork with young British Asians in Southall. Gillespie examines how her informants consume and discuss a range of media products – including soap operas, Bollywood films, televised versions of religious epics, news and global advertising – to the backdrop of their diasporic biographies (and hence the various power structures and divisions discussed thus far) in an ongoing process of sense-making, self-definition and identity construction. In doing so, British Asian young people are indeed spoken to and classified by multiple discourses of belonging, which they variously and in a context-specific manner debate, appropriate and sometimes contest. Once again, identities emerge as ongoing 'routes of becoming' (Hall 1996), multiply constrained by existing configurations of exclusion and available repertoires of shared meaning, yet subject to 'translation', creative reappropriation and the ambiguities of lives lived at the intersection of diverse influences, representations and expectations:

> [P]lural news coverages and diverse interpretations of them . . . prompt teenagers to become acutely conscious of the diversity of positions they are obliged, invited or able to choose to take up, in varying contexts, as members of internally diverse diaspora 'communities' and as British citizens. They find themselves constantly needing to ask 'Who am I?', 'Where do I speak from?' and 'Who is speaking on my behalf?' as well as 'Who is speaking to me?', and they answer these questions differently, and often ambivalently, in different circumstances. . . . This process is accelerated when, in response to dramatic public events, young people are (or feel) called upon to take explicit positions as if to resolve ambiguities and ambivalences, which, however, remain.
>
> (Gillespie 1995: 141)

The 'dramatic public events' Gillespie refers to related to news coverage of the first Gulf War. The issues she highlights have, if anything, increased in relevance since 9/11 and, particularly in a British context, since the atrocities in the London transport system in July 2005. Similar questions have been asked time and time again: What does being British Asian or British Muslim mean, if anything? Where do people's loyalties lie? Is it possible to 'live in two cultures' at the same time? Our discussion thus far already suggests that such questions are far too simplistic: they rarely pay enough attention to structural questions of inequality and exclusion, and they overlook the complexities of *all* lived identities as complex, multi-dimensional and negotiated. Such questions insist on over-simplified categories that do not square with the cultural and political 'ambiguities and ambivalences' of everyday life. Perhaps most worryingly, such questions ignore human agency, suggesting instead that individuals are fully determined by 'their culture', which in turn is misrepresented as being at odds with – as well as clearly delineated from – 'ours'. To challenge such over-simplifications we now turn to literature on hybridity.

HYBRIDITY IN THE 'DIASPORA SPACE'

Diaspora experiences occur at the intersection of different categories and are defined by the confluence of diverse cultural influences. The terms most frequently used to capture such complexity include 'hyphenated identities', cultural syncretism and, in particular, hybridity. Yasmin Hussain observes that these concepts apply to British South Asians, because they 'do not have identities . . . reducible either to one element – Britishness – or another – Asianness' (2005: 11). She makes this argument on the basis of her analysis of some of the most celebrated contributions to contemporary British cultural production (both in film and literature) that have two important things in common: first, they are the creations of British South Asian women; second, they portray identities in the terms discussed above – as ongoing 'processes of becoming' (Hall 1996), constrained by multiple 'axes' of power and inequality (Brah 1996), shaped by global and local factors, by family histories of migration and settlement, as much as by new, contextual reappropriations of diverse cultural ideas and practices. Several important issues arise from Hussain's work, including an above-mentioned methodological question about what constitutes relevant data in the sociology of ethnicity and everyday life. Put another way (and in this particular context), we are surely entitled to ask if films (such as *Bend it like Beckham*) and novels (including Meera Syal's *Anita and Me* or Monica Ali's *Brick Lane*) can advance our understanding of actual British South Asian identities. As Hussain argues convincingly, 'works of fiction [and] cinematic screenplays . . . are entirely relevant to the sociology of culture' (2005: 3): as creative reflections on lives that are always both culturally shared and idiosyncratic; not as photographic depictions, but as reflexive, inherently political and hence not infrequently controversial forms of engagement with social and cultural realities; in short, cultural production must be seen as part of its wider social and political fields, and therefore as a key arena in which identities are variously being imposed, articulated, debated, negotiated, contested and redefined.

Hussain's analysis raises two other issues that structure our discussion in the concluding section to this chapter. The first of these concerns the relationship between individuals and the different discursive practices and cultural traditions, in relation to which they live their lives; the second emphasizes that hybridity impacts on everyone inhabiting a 'diasporic space'.

Discursive negotiations

British South Asian identities can neither be described as the unconstrained synthesis of diverse cultural elements, nor – and contrary to common stereotypes – in terms of a disorientating clash of traditions and worldviews. The first generation of settlers undoubtedly experienced, as do many migrants, a 'sense of loss . . . [of] the familiar sights, sounds and smells of their birthplace' (Ballard 1994a: 9). This resonates with our conceptualization of ethnicity as, in part, the *structures of feeling* – the 'pains and pleasures, the terrors and contentments . . . the highs and humdrum of everyday lived culture' (Brah 1996: 192) – that we often only become aware of in the context of change, dislocation or crisis. Moreover, migrants-cum-settlers also found themselves confronted by various obligations that could be difficult to reconcile, such as those towards elderly parents in the subcontinent and local responsibilities towards their British-born children (e.g. Ballard 1994a: 9); their (ethnic) *structures of action* were both transnational and multi-dimensional.

Similar complexities and possible contradictions also inform the everyday worlds of second- and third-generation British South Asians. However, the much-repeated cliché of a crisis of identity, of individuals being trapped between irreconcilable cultures, does not stand up to sociological scrutiny. As we have seen, ethnicity also and importantly provides *ways of seeing*; however, individuals can and frequently do draw on very different frameworks of self-definition and interpretation in different contexts without experiencing an inevitable sense of confusion. This is well demonstrated by Roger Ballard, who compares cultures to languages, and biculturalism to bilingualism: just as human beings are able to speak two or more languages equally well, they can learn and use the conventions and symbols of different cultural traditions; particularly the descendants of (South Asian) migrants, socialized as they are into their family traditions *and* the British educational system, should be thought of as skilled 'cultural navigators', competent in – and therefore able to contextually switch between – several cultural 'codes' (Ballard 1994a: 30–33). This is not to deny that many individuals experience contradictory demands, expectations and interpretations, and that this can be a source of painful conflict. Importantly, however, Ballard challenges the common but untenable assumption that individuals are 'governed' by their cultural background, of which they can only 'have' one or risk disorientation.

The everyday negotiation of different discursive practices and the creative engagement with cultural meanings emerge with particular clarity from Gerd Baumann's above-quoted ethnography of Southall. Baumann (1996) shows that local identifications involve at least two very different understandings of identity and belonging: first, a 'dominant discourse' grounded in the British model of multiculturalism, which defines individuals as firmly grounded in – and shaped by – their respective (and reified) cultural/ethnic communities. In Southall this dominant discourse is used to distinguish between Indian and Pakistani, or more frequently Sikh, Hindu, and Muslim, as well as Afro-Caribbean, Irish and English

Southallians; serving as the main system of social classification, the dominant discourse informs much local self-understanding and sense-making and is invoked by community leaders as a mobilizing tool in the competition for scarce public resources. Baumann further observes, however, that groups and individuals also frequently oppose and deny this dominant discourse, both in their everyday lives and through alternative political alliances that cut across and contest community boundaries. Forms of alternative or 'demotic discourse' include the young generation's above-mentioned experience of British Asian-ness, local socialist and feminist networks, interfaith activities and anti-racist struggle. Thus revealing both 'culture' and 'identity' to be processes and not possessions, Baumann insists that individuals employ – and manoeuvre between – these different discourses in a context-sensitive manner:

> Southallians . . . engage not only in the dominant discourse about ethnic minorities, but also in an alternative . . . or demotic discourse about culture as a continuous process and community as a conscious creation. In this way, they command . . . a dual discursive competence. Depending upon their judgements of context and purpose, they will affirm the dominant discourse or engage the demotic, and in pitching one against the other, the very meanings of 'culture' and 'community' become the objects of social contestation.
>
> (Baumann 1996: 34–35; emphasis in original)

Baumann's notion of 'dual discursive competence' is crucial: it emphasizes that culture and ethnicity are, in part, resources contextually mobilized, reappropriated and possibly contested. However, this does not mean that such appropriations are unconstrained – which discourse is drawn upon depends on 'the perceived context, the strategies of everyday life, and the classificatory choices deemed appropriate' (Baumann 1996: 115). 'Dual discursive competence' defines social actors whose lives are lived at the intersection of various cultural traditions and structures of inclusion/exclusion, and who find themselves 'hailed into place' by several systems of classification and discursive practices; moreover, and crucially, dual discursive competence denies that such lives are prone to confusion; it stresses people's agency in negotiating possibly contradictory cultural demands and the contingencies of politics and localities.

Two-way hybridization

Hybridity is not only encountered among communities of migrants and their descendants. On the contrary, syncretism – the merging of cultural elements, ideas and practices of diverse origins – is a defining characteristic of 'diaspora spaces' in their entirety. In other words, hybridity features in all our lives. Of course, and as we have seen throughout this chapter, such diasporic spaces are structured by multiple axes of inequality (Brah 1996) and hence contain vastly different subject positions. How one experiences hybridity, whether as a source of consumerist pleasure or as a struggle with contradictory expectations, depends significantly on one's position in this matrix of power. Floya Anthias makes a similar point in warning us *not* to assume that 'cultural elements can all mix freely through the voluntaristic agency of individuals; that all cultural components are compatible . . . [or] equal in terms of power and that all subjects have equal access to the totality of cultural components' (1998: 575). Put yet another way, the mixing of cultural elements, the enjoyment or negotiation of diasporic hybridity, must be understood in its wider social contexts, which continue to be shaped by steep inequalities and multiple exclusions.

The popularity of Indian food in British society at large and the diffusion of – for example – musical genres across ethnic boundaries show that the enduring and enriching legacy of South Asian cultural elements is being acknowledged and celebrated in at least parts of the wider public sphere. Parminder Bhachu's analysis of 'London-based women entrepreneurs and designers' of the Punjabi suit (*salwaar-kameez*) provides an illuminating example of hybridity implicating – though very differently – both 'sides' of an ethnic boundary: the second-generation British South Asian producers of this increasingly popular garment *as well as* their customers, many of whom are of 'white British' background. Bhachu demonstrates that these high-street British Asian suits bear the imprints of their producers' diasporic biographies – their experiences of racism as much as their creative, everyday cultural translations and negotiations. The results are fashion designs (and philosophies) that are markedly different from their Indian-based counterparts: while the latter are informed by an anti-imperialist discourse of cultural pride and revivalism, the former involve individual customers – through a process of dialogic 'co-construction' – in the design process and exhibit what Bhachu calls 'hybridizing diasporic aesthetics':

> [S]econd generation Asian women have translated . . . domestic skills . . . into commercial domains. . . . Their diasporic sensibilities of innovation and improvisation were and are the hallmark of domestic [sewing and stitching], which is encoded in their highly negotiative entrepreneurship of co-construction of clothes they sell to their customers in their London shops.
>
> (Bhachu 2005: 45)

These diasporic fashion designers therefore incorporate their customers' own ideas through the creative fusion of diverse cultural styles and elements. In the process, 'new forms of Britishness and Europeanness' (Bhachu 2005: 54) are being generated, through the adaptable medium of the *salwaar-kameez* and thanks to the diasporic agency and cultural sensitivity of second-generation British Asian women.

British cinematic and literary cultural production has also been greatly enriched by South Asian influences. Yasmin Hussain thus speaks of a contemporary 'desification' of British cinema. *Desi* meaning 'authentically South Asian', this refers to – for example – Gurinder Chadha's popular films *Bhaji on the Beach* (1994) and *Bend it like Beckham* (2002). In addition to their commercial success, these and similar films (as well as novels) are both culturally and politically highly significant: first, insofar as they portray and challenge the continuing effects of (everyday) racism; second, because they highlight 'differences and conflicts . . . not only between but also within cultural groups', thus helping to deconstruct homogenizing stereotypes of both the self and other; third (and most immediately relevant to our present discussion), they amount to a 're-definition of British identities as susceptible to movement and change . . . a hybridization of identity' (Hussain 2005: 10, 16). In other words, certain forms of critical (British South Asian) cultural production confirm that identity labels or subject positions, including 'Britishness', are subject to historical change, cultural diversification and the ambivalences of everyday life.

CONCLUSION

This chapter has examined ethnicity and everyday life as manifest in the articulation, experience, reappropriation and at times contestation of British South Asian identities. Stuart Hall's definition of identities as 'ongoing projects of becoming' significantly constrained but not wholly determined by multiple power structures and their discursive practices has served as a theoretical lead. Identities, Hall argues, are only ever temporary 'meeting points' between power and discourse on the one hand, and an individual's (psychic) investment in the 'subject position' they are 'allocated' on the other. Historical change, ideological contestation and individual agency are all acknowledged by such a conceptualization of identities. As we have seen, this 'model' also illuminates the complex diversities of diasporic South Asian identities and their continuous negotiation in relation to multiple systems of exclusion and inequality, both across and within community boundaries.

Everyday life implicates changing historical contexts, structural constraints and possible resistance to them, as well as reflexivity or its absence. By way of conclusion to this chapter I would like to briefly draw attention to an empirical snapshot of a particular discourse of British Asian identity, in which these three dimensions may be observed to intersect: the snapshot in question was provided by the editor's letter in a popular British Asian women's magazine published soon after the 7/7 bombings in London. The letter (Shetty 2005: 5) started by stating that 'there are enough stresses in a modern British Asian woman's life . . . without you having to pick up your favourite magazine just to read: *sorry hun, things are pretty tough.*' Having defined its audience, the editor thus arguably made reference to the many *structures of action* within which British Asian women's lives are lived. In such a context (and as a form of reflexivity), the magazine's aims were defined as including 'bringing serious issues to light and tackling difficult taboos', yet ultimately to 'leave the reader with a positive message'. The effects of 'history' on everyday life then took centre stage: 'But then the bombs went off.' The many tragic consequences of the London bombings included an increase in racial hostility and suspicion. The likely impact of this on the magazine's audience emerged from the subsequent observation that 'there isn't a single person reading this who hasn't been left shaken . . . and fearful of what the future might hold'. In accordance with the magazine's objectives, the editor went on to articulate an optimistic message, informed by a unifying discourse of British Asian-ness: 'Life is not going to get harder as a result of these mindless atrocities. If anything, it will make us grow stronger. Asiana is a place where your respective religion and background are of no consequence.'

There is a continuing tendency in much public discourse to assume that the everyday lives, pleasures and preoccupations of different communities are hermetically sealed from one another, that the values and practices of one community are radically different from others'. Making a necessary mockery of such assumptions, the editor's conclusion provides an insight into how ethnic identities need to be understood in their wider social and historical contexts:

> Here, all we care about is that you love the best of all things British Asian – our unique way of life, our hot celebrities, our brilliant fashion and, of course, our gorgeous men!
>
> (Shetty 2005: 5)

Clearly, the 'late modern' preoccupations with consumerism and celebrities are shared, by some, across ethnic boundaries. That said, other discourses articulated in parts of the South Asian diaspora (as elsewhere) define themselves in outright opposition to such concerns, insisting on exclusive and rigid identities, and claiming to react against such 'signs of our times'. Taken together, these contrasting discourses arguably provide the end-points of an ideological continuum along which identities are continuously being articulated, debated, redefined, lived and contested. As we have seen, simplistic divisions between 'us' and 'them' severely distort social realities. Moreover, stereotypes contribute significantly to, and often exacerbate, the risks and dangers that ultimately we all confront and need to address together. Above and beyond the specificities of any one case study, understanding ethnicity and everyday life requires an engagement with some universal social phenomena: identities, while very significantly shaped by existing traditions and structures of inequality, also involve individuals with some – though inevitably constrained – agency.

4

ETHNIC MAJORITIES, 'THE STRANGER' AND EVERYDAY LIFE

The general insights provided by Chapters 2 and 3 include the observation that ethnicity is – at least in part – constructed across, and as an expression of, social boundaries. Processes of boundary construction and maintenance inevitably include some people and exclude others; they are, by definition, articulations of (cultural) difference with political consequences. Put another way, our discussion thus far has shown that ethnicity implicates the relatively disempowered, marginalized or excluded *as well as* dominant social groups and institutions. Ethnicity, we might argue, matters particularly in contexts of inequality between groups widely considered to constitute 'the cultural majority' and those living as minorities respectively.

This observation also echoes an introductory point made in Chapter 1: discourses of national and ethnic belonging share some important family characteristics including the construction of boundaries (and their tangible political consequences), as well as the postulate that the communities in question exhibit – despite internal differences of power, status and wealth – 'group comradeship' based on culture and nationality respectively. In this chapter, I explore the similarities between notions of national and ethnic belonging in greater detail. In doing so, I challenge the common but sociologically problematic assumption that ethnicity defines numerical, cultural minorities only. Instead, we need to also account for powerful 'ethnic majorities' (e.g. Fenton 2003: 160) that define themselves with reference to (by now familiar) markers such as descent and culture. If promoted and utilized by state institutions, cultural/ethnic characteristics such as language, historical memories or ancestry can become criteria for inclusion in the 'national community'. In other words, the difference between national majorities and ethnic minorities is one of power and not the respective absence or presence of ethnicity.

The case study for this chapter, contemporary Austria, has been widely portrayed as a paradigmatic instance of a defining characteristic of today's world: the renewed appeal of discourses of ethno-national belonging and exclusion. While such discourses are highly pertinent to our discussion insofar as they delineate clear boundaries between the 'national self' and various excluded others, they do not tell the whole story. Drawing on sociological debates about 'the stranger', I distinguish between various dominant and alternative/critical responses to, and conceptualizations of, ethnic otherness as encountered in Austrian politics, civil society and cultural production. I thereby show that the boundaries between ethnic majorities and 'the stranger' are subject to considerable ideological contestation, giving rise to competing discourses of relative exclusion, assimilation and pluralism. Moreover, I argue that the realm of everyday life, its historical specificities and political reflexivity within it, are crucial to such ongoing discursive struggles.

RESPONSES TO 'THE STRANGER'

I have argued that among the defining characteristics of ethnicity is its provision of *ways of seeing* the world. Furthermore, I have stressed that such shared frameworks of interpretation are among the discursive practices that create subject positions; in other words, ethnicity makes certain identities possible by delineating a cultural 'self' from various 'others'. As we have also seen, however, such identity discourses are subject to historical change, internal disagreement and resistance. Having discussed identity negotiations among communities of migrants and their descendants in the previous chapter, we now examine – though again inevitably briefly – various constructions of ethnic sameness and otherness as internally contested *ways of seeing* the world encountered among a dominant majority. The broader theoretical questions addressed in this chapter include the following: since all identities rely on self–other distinctions, how is *the relationship* between self and other defined by politicians, in the media, by dominant social groups, national elites and ethnic majorities (see also Baumann and Gingrich 2004)? What alternative relationships between self and other are also being articulated, by whom and where? In other words, this is a discussion of the everyday politics of classification among an ethnic majority.

The question of how dominant groups and institutions conceptualize and respond to ethnic otherness emerges from parts of Zygmunt Bauman's work (1990, 1993). Bauman observes that modern nation states have been preoccupied with internal cultural homogeneity, which requires strategies for dealing with the inherent ambivalence of 'the stranger'. The latter was first defined, by the great German sociologist Georg Simmel, as a person 'who comes today and stays tomorrow' and hence embodies difference in 'our' midst (Bauman 1990: 149). In a closely related vein, Bauman turns to a distinction between two societal responses to the stranger's 'otherness' first introduced by the French anthropologist Claude Lévi-Strauss: *anthropoemic* strategies of removal or permanent exclusion, and *anthropophagic* strategies of 'ingestion', assimilation and hence transformation of otherness into sameness respectively. *Anthropoemic* responses to the stranger thus draw rigid and permanent boundaries between self and other, define them as mutually exclusive and irreconcilably different categories, and maintain social difference and political separation between them. On the other hand, *anthropophagic* responses insist that others become 'like us', take on 'our characteristics' and hence merge into an assumed 'cultural mainstream'. Crucially (and unlike Lévi-Strauss), Bauman also observes that these two contrasting strategies do not characterize different types of societies, but *co-exist within* all social formations, 'are applied in parallel, in each society and on every level of social organization' (1993: 163). It is indeed tempting to map contemporary political responses to (cultural) otherness on to this ideal-typical distinction between *anthropoemic* and *anthropophagic* strategies and to also corroborate Bauman's observation that they are applied and articulated alongside one another. We merely need to think of the multiple narratives that surround all of us living inside (or indeed beyond) 'Fortress Europe' and that address the otherness allegedly epitomized by asylum seekers and refugees (as much as by long-established communities of migrants-cum-settlers); such discourses (and certain related policies) do indeed variously exclude the other by means as varied as the perpetuation of social/legal inequalities and physical deportation, or demand its complete cultural assimilation.

In this chapter, I turn to contemporary Austria as a part of 'Fortress Europe' whose responses to, and constructions of, otherness have in recent years come under (national and international) scrutiny and debate. This happened in particular following the inclusion of the far right Austrian Freedom Party (FPÖ), formerly headed by Jörg Haider, in a coalition government with the Austrian People's Party (ÖVP) in February 2000, to which the country's then fourteen EU partners responded by imposing a series of temporary 'sanctions' on Austria. In what follows I partly corroborate and partly qualify Bauman's observation concerning the co-existence of *anthropoemic* and *anthropophagic* responses to 'the stranger': while they indeed sit alongside one another in much public discourse, we will also discover evidence of other ways of defining and critically re-conceptualizing the relationship between the (Austrian) national self and various ethnic others. Moreover, such competing discourses are more than alternative ways of classifying the social world. They have political implications insofar as they engage with existing power relations; drawing on Antonio Gramsci's terminology, I begin by discussing 'hegemonic' discourses (i.e. *anthropoemic, anthropophagic* and others) that justify and help reproduce existing configurations of power, both on national and pan-European levels. I then discuss select examples of 'counter-hegemonic' discourses that challenge existing inequalities and exclusions either by celebrating cultural pluralism or by questioning the very distinction between an ethnic/national self and 'the other'. I will argue that understanding both hegemonic and counter-hegemonic discourses requires an engagement with everyday life, its historically variable characteristics and the role of power, resistance and reflexivity within it.

This chapter resembles the previous ones in two respects: first, in presenting and analysing a specific case study (i.e. contemporary

Austria), the historical particularities of which we turn to next; and second, in emphasizing that beyond the specificities of a case study there are more general points and observations to be made. In this chapter, the more general issues relate to the position and lives of 'strangers' inside 'Fortress Europe', to the ideological struggles among ethnic majorities as to how and where the boundaries delineating the 'national community' are to be drawn, and as to how permeable those boundaries are or should be. In drawing on different forms of data as 'discursive snapshots' indicative of competing ways of defining the 'self' and 'others', we also revisit more general questions concerning the politics of cultural production and everyday life.

A BRIEF AND RECENT HISTORY OF THE 'ALPINE REPUBLIC'

Located in the heart of Europe, Austria's twentieth-century history was profoundly shaped by the continent's crises, conflicts, wars and tragedies, times of turmoil as well as subsequent reconstruction and prosperity during that period. Following the end of World War I and the disintegration of the multi-ethnic Habsburg empire in 1918, the largely German-speaking First Austrian Republic soon found itself beset by severe economic difficulties and polarization between the forces of the political Right and the Left. Continuing crises in the 1930s culminated at first in authoritarian, one-party rule and subsequently, in 1938, in the unresisted annexation of Austria by Hitler Germany. This was followed by the country's (and the entire continent's) darkest historical chapter – World War II and the Holocaust. As we shall see, Austria's dual 'role' of both 'perpetrator and victim' (e.g. Sully 1990) in the period 1938 to 1945 – epitomized by willing participants in the horrendous crimes committed under Nazism and by the persecution, dispossession, expulsion and mass-murder of those constructed as its ideological 'others' respectively – plays an important role in contemporary debates about national identity, history and ethnic diversity. However, widespread critical engagement with the country's World War II history is a relatively recent phenomenon (e.g. Pelinka and Weinzierl 1987; Botz and Sprengnagel 1994; Wassermann 2002).

Economic and political reconstruction in the post-war period, which had begun under allied military occupation between 1945 and 1955, crucially involved a newly dominant and particularistic discourse of national identity. In contrast to the previous pervasiveness of a pan-Germanic self-understanding, Austria's cultural and historical separateness now came to be emphasized and celebrated (e.g. Thaler 2001; Karner 2005b). In the process, however, a highly selective historical (mis-)construction of Austria as 'Hitler's first victim' also gained ground and delayed critical engagement with the Holocaust among many Austrians (e.g. Sully 1990; Bischof 1993).

Significantly, the decades following the end of World War II were characterized by the country's 'economic miracle', increasing affluence, a political system of somewhat extraordinary stability and durability based on consensual democracy, a strong welfare state, and the systematic sharing of power between the two dominant parties – the Social Democrats (SPÖ) and the Centre-Right Austrian People's Party (ÖVP). It was not until the 1980s that Austria's international image and self-perception as an 'island of the blessed' started to erode. Numerous factors then converged and contributed to a new climate of political controversy, uncertainty, debate and far-reaching structural change (e.g. Pelinka 1990, 1998): these included increasing disgruntlement with established political structures, the fall of communism beyond Austria's eastern borders and the war in former Yugoslavia contributing to demographic changes through immigration; the growing inescapability of the forces of economic globalization, which also contributed to the decision to join the European Union in 1995; and the international controversies surrounding the presidential election of former UN general secretary Kurt Waldheim in 1986 on the one hand, and Jörg Haider's rise to political prominence on the other. Sociologically significant about both of these controversies was the fact that Austria's World War II past was now brought to the forefront of public consciousness – in the course of debates about Waldheim's former role in the German army and against the backdrop of some highly controversial statements made by Haider about the Nazi era and the Austrian nation (see e.g. Haslinger 1995). The increasing mobilizing power of Haider's neo-nationalism during the 1990s is often explained with reference to two of its key characteristics: first, its discourse of a nation allegedly threatened by immigration (e.g. Wodak 2000), which began to appeal to many in times of rapid domestic and international social change; second, and arguably more importantly, its articulation of widespread discontent with existing structures of power and decision-making (e.g. Pelinka 2000: 56–57). An analysis of contemporary Austria requires an engagement with wider historical contexts, recent political transformations and global economic changes. Reactions to this period of accelerated social change have, as we shall see, been varied.

Competing reactions to change and crisis

We have, at several points in our discussion, raised questions concerning the effects of crises on ethnic identities and everyday life. Following Pierre Bourdieu (1977), I have suggested that experiences of rapid and often anxiety-inducing social change can transform previously taken-for-granted cultural meanings and practices into consciously articulated 'ethnic ideologies' (Vertovec 2000). Crises, Bourdieu observes, have the capacity to instil reflection on things that previously appeared self-evident, to transform a cultural *habitus* into a realm of discourse, debate and disagreement. Along with the rest of the world, Austria has – over the past two decades – experienced far-reaching structural changes. Not only have the latter impacted on everyday life, but they have also triggered reflection and discussion. Ethno-nationalism, however, has merely been one among several competing reactions to the experience of multiple crises and social transformations.

Based on an analysis of the country's main print media, I have elsewhere argued (Karner 2005a) that Bourdieu's model of the crisis-induced transformation of a previously 'undiscussed' universe of cultural common sense (or *doxa*) into a terrain of contested discourses captures important parts of recent Austrian history. Various surveys conducted towards the end of the period of relative political stability from the mid-1950s to the mid-1980s had revealed a number of core symbols of Austrian national identity including its 'scenic beauty' and environment, key historical and artistic personalities, its political institutions, food, people and language (e.g. Reiterer 1988; Bruckmüller 1996 [1984]). Revealingly, however, recent years have

seen controversies and developments that have presented several of
these important but previously largely taken-for-granted markers of
national identity with crises. Some such crises could be counted
among the local symptoms of globalization including the environmental impact of European lorries transiting the country or the
closure of factories by their multinational owners in search of
lower labour costs elsewhere (and against the backdrop of rising
national unemployment figures); other crises, while also among
the mediated effects of globalization, directly affected everyday
objects and practices: these included the once planned EU-wide
standardization of labels on jam jars (which would have replaced a
distinctly Austrian-German term with its northern German
equivalent), fears articulated in parts of the tabloid press that
transnational media networks were eroding peculiarly Austrian
dialects and colloquialisms, and a cross-border controversy following
the inclusion of artists and composers widely associated with Austria
on a list of 'great historical Germans' in the German media. Crucially,
however, the reactions to these crises affecting symbols of national
identity were heterogeneous rather than monolithic; ethno-
nationalist demands to protect 'our' language, food, environment or
history were thus internally contested by alternative accounts that
variously pointed at the inevitability of cultural and linguistic
change, at home-grown contributions to air pollution, the benefits
of the European market to the Austrian economy, and at the multi-
dimensionality of everyone's – including, say, Mozart's – identities
(Karner 2005a).

   In what follows, I move the discussion back towards the question
of how and where discursive and institutional boundaries separating dominant majorities from ethnic minorities are variously
constructed, maintained, debated, contested and negotiated. In
doing so, I emphasize the significance of everyday life – its politics
and its cultural hybridity – to such ideological struggles. It must be
noted, however, that I can here merely *record* the co-existence of
competing discourses of identity and their contrasting definitions of
the self–other relationship. Constraints of space do not allow for a
thorough examination of their relative salience among a population
of eight million people. The intention, then, is to draw attention to
discursive struggles over group classifications within an ethnic

majority and to cast some light on the role of the everyday in such struggles.

HEGEMONIC DIVERSITY

Let us recap: nation states tend to promote cultural homogeneity, which can put strangers – those who 'come today and stay tomorrow' – into precarious positions. The two strategies of *anthropoemic* (i.e. exclusion) and *anthropophagic* (i.e. assimilation) responses are, according to Zygmunt Bauman, always applied in parallel. Moreover, both responses tend to be hegemonic insofar as they help to reproduce existing configurations of power. In times of modernity, the latter were predominantly organized by, and around, the nation state. As modernity turns into something else ('late', 'second' or 'liquid modernity', depending on our preferred theoretical lead), power – though still significantly invested in state structures – is also organized in transnational 'network states' (Castells 1998) such as the European Union and, importantly, exercised by economic actors such as multinational corporations. Consequently, hegemonic activity no longer merely serves to reproduce national but also transnational, and global/economic power. Debates about migration, ageing populations, asylum seekers, human rights, 'Fortress Europe' (or any other fortress, for that matter) show that the question as to how strangers are conceptualized and responded to is an extremely important and timely one. Returning to our current case study, it is possible to discern not only *anthropoemic* and *anthropophagic* responses but also other suggested self–other relationships.

Anthropoemic and anthropophagic responses

Anthropoemic and *anthropophagic* responses to 'the stranger' share some common conceptual ground insofar as they both clearly distinguish between an ethnic/national self and various others. However, they differ fundamentally in their subsequent responses to cultural difference: *anthropoemic* responses preserve and institutionalize difference, as reflected in discourses about *primordial*, one-dimensional and unchanging identities as well as in policies of exclusion; by contrast, *anthropophagic* responses aim at the erasure of difference by means of the other's assimilation into an imputed national mainstream. As already mentioned, 'Fortress Europe' abounds with versions of both strategies and, indeed, their co-existence.

In an Austrian context, evidence of *anthropoemic* responses among parts of the ethnic majority emerge from nationalist rhetoric, in which a 'black-and-white' worldview constructs 'good' in-groups and 'bad' out-groups, separating 'us' from 'them' (Wodak 2000: 180). The thereby created dichotomy delineates 'real Austrians' from 'foreigners and asylum seekers' who find themselves discursively reified and institutionally excluded. This is further illuminated in Martin Reisigl and Ruth Wodak's detailed linguistic analysis of a variety of relevant political statements, texts and documents that assume 'polarizations, black-and-white portrayals and manichean divisions into good and bad', give rise to 'a sharp "us" and "them" pattern' and 'construct a world of "insiders" and "outsiders"' (2001: 56, 96, 105). However, the construction and reproduction of the national 'self' occurs not only through political rhetoric and explicit identity politics but also – though less reflexively – in the realm of the everyday: in Austria, this has been shown to involve a range of linguistic devices that create 'national sameness' by invoking ideas about a common national culture, a 'national body', a shared (political) history and the idea of a distinctly Austrian personality type (De Cillia *et al.* 1999: 158–164). Providing examples of 'banal nationalism' (Billig 1995), such everyday notions and rhetoric also clearly separate 'us' from 'them', defining a version of national identity through difference and exclusion. A recent survey suggested that *anthropoemic* notions of far-reaching and persisting cultural differences are indeed relatively widespread (and I would again argue that this is indicative of pan-European trends and not peculiar to Austria), with 65 per cent of respondents defining immigrants as a 'burden', an assessment made particularly often of sub-Saharan asylum seekers and refugees (www.orf.at, 16 September 2004).

However, the same survey also provided corroborating evidence for Bauman's argument that *anthropoemic* and *anthropophagic* responses to 'the stranger' tend to be applied alongside one another: 81 per cent of respondents thus agreed with the suggestion that cultural/ linguistic 'integration' should be demanded of settlers in Austria (www.orf.at, 16 September 2004). As revealingly *anthropophagic* was a relatively recent and controversial piece of legislation – the so-called Integration Act (*Integrationsvertrag*) that sought to define compulsory German language courses as a prerequisite for renewing (non-EU) immigrants' residence permits; while this was an obvious instance of institutionalized *anthropophagic* thought and practice, it is also worth noting that large numbers of successfully claimed exemptions made its 'effectiveness' somewhat debatable (www.orf.at, 26 January 2004).

Dominant majorities thus respond to 'the stranger' not only by talking to or about them but also through a range of institutional mechanisms that variously effect their exclusion (if *anthropoemic*) or assimilation (if *anthropophagic*). Ethnicity, I have argued, provides some of the *structures of action* that significantly shape (though do not fully determine) people's routine behaviour and long-term life trajectories. In the case of ethnic majorities, it tends to be political elites and state institutions that provide comparable *structures of action*, making certain practices more likely or possible for those under their jurisdiction and legislative 'reach' than for those outside it. A key mechanism in this process is the principle of citizenship. The Austrian case is interesting in this context, since it incorporates both *anthropoemic* and *anthropophagic* elements while also providing evidence of internal contestation of institutionally enshrined self–other boundaries. That said, comparable discussions and exclusions are – of course – encountered across the world. Moreover, the current discussion must be seen in its wider context – that of the European Union, where citizenship crucially defines individuals' *structures of action*, their ability to move, work and vote within the EU; in other words, whether one is able to enjoy EU privileges or be excluded from them depends – for many people and at least in the first instance – on the type of passport one holds.

Austrian citizenship law is broadly based on the principle of descent (or *ius sanguinis*); in other words, citizenship is conferred on the basis of a parent's citizenship. This stands in contrast to *ius soli*, whereby place of birth – rather than ancestry – is the criterion of inclusion in the 'national community'. These contrasting models of citizenship are widely associated with two alternative definitions of national belonging (e.g. McCrone 1998; Karner 2005b): ethnic nationalism (broadly comparable with *ius sanguinis*), which includes only people *born into* a cultural/national community; and, conversely, civic or territorial nationalism (analogous to *ius soli*), which bestows membership to everyone *born on* the territory of the nation state in question. In the terms of the current discussion, *ius sanguinis* is broadly *anthropoemic* in character insofar as it draws more or less permanent boundaries by virtue of birth/descent and hence effects relatively enduring exclusions of the cultural other. *Ius soli*, by contrast, favours cultural assimilation and is therefore *anthropophagic* in orientation. Revealingly, however, the case of Austrian citizenship – and despite its general/historical adherence to the *anthropoemic* descent principle – provides further evidence of the two strategies being applied in parallel. This emerged from a recent amendment to citizenship legislation: as before, the most common route for non-Austrians to apply for citizenship is after ten years of legal residence in the country; however, applicants now also need to be economically secure and – in *anthropophagic* fashion – are required to pass a German language test (www.orf.at, 6 December 2005). Crucially, it should also be noted that existing citizenship legislation has been a source of controversy for a while, with parts of the (at the time of writing) political opposition declaring a preference for *ius soli* and articulating strong criticisms of these recent amendments (e.g. www.orf.at, 25 August 2005, http://derstandard.at, 26 September 2005). Once again we thus encounter evidence of social, in this case institutionally guarded, boundaries being subject to (internal) contestation and possible historical redefinition.

Degrees of otherness

Our discussion has so far corroborated Zygmunt Bauman's observation that strategies of exclusion and assimilation co-exist, and are applied in parallel, within any one social formation and in its varied responses to cultural otherness. However, a closer look at Austria – and, one suspects, most other contemporary contexts – reveals that national identities can also be conceptualized differently. The assumed relationship between the categories of self and other is thus also defined, on occasion, in a distinctly hierarchical manner with degrees of assumed similarity characterizing the relationship between the central category of the 'national community' and various other national/ethnic groupings. 'We', one might paraphrase the 'grammar of identity' (Baumann and Gingrich 2004) informing this alternative *way of seeing and classifying* the world, also consider ourselves to be a little like 'them', even more like 'this group', but really very different from 'those over there'.

Evidence of such assumed degrees of otherness is provided by Reisigl and Wodak (2001: 62), who record the 'discursive construction of a hierarchy of foreigners' in everyday discourse, on the basis of which non-Austrians from the European Economic Area are often favourably (albeit implicitly) distinguished from foreigners from outside the EEA. Earlier quantitative studies on perceptions of relative likeness partly complicate this picture by suggesting that many Austrians' ideas of 'national similarity' tap into geographical proximity and contemporary political configurations only alongside linguistic connections, (perceived) cultural affinity and older historical ties. The above-mentioned, in the post-war era increasingly prominent and dominant discourse of Austrian particularism, which had replaced previously common ideas of pan-Germanic belonging (e.g. Hanisch 1994; Thaler 2001), thus sits alongside notions of relative cross-border likeness. This emerged from a survey conducted in early 1990, in which a nationally representative sample defined former West Germany as Austria's 'closest relative', followed by Hungary, Switzerland, former Czechoslovakia, former East Germany and Slovenia; by contrast, Italy, Croatia, Serbia, Poland and Romania were – in this order – defined as the culturally most alien countries in Austria's relative geographical proximity (Pelinka 1990: 139). In an earlier study respondents had ranked Germans, Swiss, Hungarians, Czechs, Yugoslavs, Italians, Americans and Russians in descending order of 'national similarity' to Austrians (though these findings varied considerably with class and educational backgrounds); in yet another survey about people's main source of identification, 20 per cent of respondents identified Austria, 19 per cent their particular locality, 12 per cent their region, 2 per cent Europe, 1 per cent an assumed pan-Germanic entity, and 45 per cent a universalist conception of 'humanity' (Reiterer 1988: 122, 37–38).

As with all identity discourses (see Chapter 3), such findings need to be contextualized: we are therefore justified in querying if, for example, universalist identifications with 'humanity' are borne out by people's everyday lives and the self-definitions they may articulate elsewhere. Moreover, these findings are of course also subject to historical change; thus discourses of European identity have certainly become considerably more widespread since the above-quoted surveys were conducted and particularly since Austria joined the EU in 1995 (recent and renewed Euro-scepticism notwithstanding). None the less, these surveys make a very pertinent point about self–other boundaries and their negotiation within ethnic majorities: they show that the construction of Austrian national identities does not rely on *anthropoemic* and *anthropophagic* strategies only but that it also involves – very significantly in some contexts – notions of graded, rather than singular and absolute, otherness. Moreover, historical comparison reveals changing patterns of perceived similarities: between the late 1980s and the mid-1990s the percentage of Austrians emphasizing national likeness *vis-à-vis* Germany and Switzerland declined relative to an increasing assertion of cultural relatedness to Hungary (Bruckmüller 1996 [1984]: 136); this must be seen in its historical context – the fall of the iron curtain making the subsequent public re-discovery of a central European 'space' possible. Ulram and Tributsch similarly observe that while seven out of ten Austrians identified Germany as culturally 'most alike' in 1980, the end of the Cold War made older historical connections with Hungary – and to a lesser extent the Czech Republic – more real and pronounced. Subsequently, Austria's EU membership again strengthened political and economic ties to Germany; however, when in 2000 – following the controversial inclusion of the far Right Austrian Freedom Party (FPÖ) in a coalition government – her then fourteen EU partners imposed a series of temporary 'sanctions' on Austria, EU scepticism grew and public sympathies in the Alpine Republic changed again – 'in favour' of Switzerland and Hungary and to the detriment of Austro-German 'relations' (Ulram and Tributsch 2004: 42–45).

Focusing on a particular national context, this chapter has so far demonstrated that institutional and discursive responses to 'the stranger' include *anthropoemic*, *anthropophagic*, as well as 'grading' strategies and that the perceived boundaries defining ethnic majorities are subject to (internal) debate, negotiation and change. In what follows, we shift our attention to select contributions to the sphere of Austrian cultural production, which critically engage with a variety of issues: Austrian history; the position of ethnic minorities inside 'Fortress Europe'; the cultural hybridity of biographies and everyday lives, which challenge rigid ethnic boundaries drawn by parts of the dominant majority.

PLURALISM AND COUNTER-HEGEMONY

Our conceptual focus in this chapter thus far has been on the construction and reproduction of self–other distinctions through *structures of action* and *ways of seeing* among dominant ethnic majorities. At the same time, I have stressed throughout this book that despite the constraints imposed by the former and the apparent plausibility of the latter, human agency and reflexivity mean that power structures as well as dominant ways of classifying and interpreting the world are subject to debate, negotiation and potential resistance. As we shall see in the remainder of this chapter, such processes and ideological alternatives can also challenge the assumed relationship between self and other, between ethnic majorities and 'the stranger'. In an Austrian context, the realm of cultural production – by which I refer to a range of signifying practices that include literature, critical journalism and music – plays a key role in such political debates about boundaries and exclusion/inclusion. The discursive alternatives encountered in what follows oppose both *anthropoemic* and *anthropophagic* responses to 'the stranger', while also avoiding the common hierarchies of cultural similarity discussed in the previous section. Two critical alternatives may be discerned: first, a logic of pluralism, which – rather than effecting the other's exclusion or demanding its assimilation – celebrates and seeks to preserve cultural diversity; second, a form of counter-hegemony, which questions the very distinction between self and other. As we shall see, the first alternative builds on a reflexive, critical engagement with (Austrian) history, while the second alternative uses the cultural ambivalence of everyday life to deconstruct and challenge systems of ethnic classification and exclusion. It must be stressed again that, given limitations of space, the following discussion needs to be highly selective and allows me only to discuss a series of discursive snapshots; consequently, it is my aim merely to draw attention to a realm of civil society and cultural production, in which alternatives to the *anthropoemic* and *anthropophagic* strategies of exclusion and assimilation are articulated and debated.

Critical pluralism

The significance of World War II and the Holocaust, the Nazis' systematic mass-murder of some six million Jews and other categories of people they considered 'subhuman', as the darkest chapter in both Austrian and wider European history, has already been mentioned. Erika Weinzierl summarizes its Austrian dimensions as follows: prior to World War II, Vienna had the largest Jewish population in the German-speaking world; during the Holocaust, 65,459 Austrian Jews were murdered, 128,500 others escaped into exile; conversely, the proportion of Austrians among the perpetrators of the Holocaust was 'not small' (Weinzierl 1997: 55, 93–95). The unprecedented horror and scale of the crimes committed under Nazism provide the most infamous illustration of what is at stake in the relationship between dominant majorities and ethnic minorities. A watershed in human history, the Holocaust revealed the depths of cruelty and inhumanity which social classification and political 'responses' to ideologically constructed 'strangers' can entail.

It has often been pointed out that Austrian post-war society was slow in confronting the Holocaust and its centrality in recent Austrian history, preferring instead to uphold the myth that it had solely been 'Hitler's first victim' rather than simultaneously victim and perpetrator (e.g. Sully 1990). While there were always pockets of critical discussion about Austria's recent past (see e.g. Adunka 2002: 17–19, 29–33), it was arguably only in the context of the above-mentioned political controversies surrounding Kurt Waldheim and Jörg Haider that more widespread critical engagement with the country's World War II history started to take hold. Prior to that, it was mainly artists and writers who criticized – sometimes to considerable public outcry – what they saw as a disconcerting lack of discussion about the Holocaust. More recently, political initiatives and public opinion have followed suit: successive

Austrian governments have put 'emphasis on education to achieve greater knowledge and awareness of the Holocaust . . . school books have been rewritten, anti-Semitism has been decried, a national fund was established for the benefit of Jewish survivors . . . [and] restitution claims are handled expeditiously' (Pick 2000: 201). That said, grass-root responses to this period of intensified public historical reflections have been varied. On one end of the spectrum and among a right-leaning minority, there has been continuing reluctance to critically confront the country's World War II past coupled with persisting anti-Semitic prejudice; on the other end and nowadays among the majority, the importance of a self-critical engagement with the Holocaust is acknowledged and stressed (Weinzierl 1997: 244–247). Moreover, a cultural pluralism informed by critical reflections on the Holocaust is captured by important contributions to public discourse: for example, the weekly paper *Profil* recently reported (Steinitz 2006) on the still comparatively small Jewish community in contemporary Austria, its growing vitality and self-confidence, its ethnic distinctiveness, internal diversity and historical consciousness; its self-understanding was portrayed as informed by religious tradition, the Holocaust and contemporary multi-culturalism, giving rise to complex identities and cosmopolitan everyday lives that are *both* Jewish *and* Austrian, successfully resisting *anthropoemic* exclusion as well as *anthropophagic* assimilation.

I earlier justified my choice of case study for this chapter by pointing out that contemporary Austria is widely considered to be a typical example of the recent rise of ethno-nationalist politics observed across large parts of the globe. More accurately, nationalist politics in Austria provides – despite its for some time extraordinary electoral success – some more general lessons about the mobilizing potential of exclusions, fears and anxieties across and beyond 'Fortress Europe' (e.g. Hainsworth 2000; Camus 2002). That being said, my main aim here is to show that the drawing of rigidly nationalist boundaries is only one among several competing reactions to a recent and continuing period of rapid social change and perceived (economic as well as cultural) crises. In other words, there are alternative discursive reactions to contemporary problems; such critical alternatives include versions of cultural pluralism, which oppose nationalist identity politics and everyday racism, challenge the structural exclusion of 'strangers' in 'Fortress Europe', and celebrate ethnic otherness instead of advocating its exclusion or assimilation (see Karner 2007). While such pluralist discourses may be seen in their wider context of transnational civil societies, some Austrian contributions to critical pan-European debates continue to be shaped by the scars of Austrian history; thus, for example, contemporary racism is in certain forms of cultural production interpreted as an indication that the lessons of World War II and the Holocaust still remain to be fully absorbed.

One manifestation of this critical discourse was provided by the (formerly) often controversial Austrian writer and recent Nobel prize winner Elfriede Jelinek. Her play *Stecken, Stab und Stangl* was written in the aftermath of the terrible murder of four Romani men in the eastern region of Burgenland in February 1995; the four men were killed in a vicious racist attack – by explosives wired to a sign reading 'Gypsies go back to India', which they were trying to remove. Jelinek's motivation for writing *Stecken, Stab und Stangl* has been quoted as follows:

> I wanted to offer this terribly oppressed minority, which lives in horrendous conditions . . . the utmost of what I have accomplished in my art. It is for those without a voice or whose language we don't understand.
>
> (Jelinek, cited in Kosta 2003: 82)

In terms of the current discussion, Jelinek obviously addresses the boundaries and relations between the sedentary 'us', the powerful ethnic majority and silenced, excluded Roma minorities. As we saw in Chapter 2, Romani history has been partly defined by external mechanisms of power and oppression, and the contemporary era shows few signs that this is about to change anywhere. As such, Jelinek's play addresses an issue of undeniably transnational, near-global relevance. At the same time, however, her focus – in challenging the marginalization endured by the Roma as well as the wider historical conditions of possibly underpinning xenophobia and racism – lies on Austria: *Stecken, Stab und Stangl* has been interpreted as an attempt to confront Austria's World War II past and 'its persistence . . . [in] the linguistic fabrication of the imagined [national] community' (Kosta 2003: 96). The play challenges everyday preoccupations with consumerism and sport, ethnically exclusive notions of 'tradition', and – crucially – the influence of Austria's largest (tabloid) newspaper (see also Mayer and Koberg 2006: 210–212). Jelinek's criticism is, in part, directed at what is portrayed as a (among some sections) continuing reluctance to mourn the victims of the Holocaust; this is reflected in various characters' repeated declarations that 'enough is enough' (*Einmal muß Schluß sein*), which echo far Right calls to put an end to self-critical historical reflections and to restitution claims by Holocaust survivors and victims' descendants. Connecting the country's past to the present, Jelinek's play crucially objects to both *anthropoemic* and *anthropophagic* responses to 'cultural strangers': her opposition to the former emerges from her portrayal of characters calling on the four murdered Roma men – in chilling intertextual references to the wired sign they were trying to remove – to 'return to India' as well as from another shady character's declaration that 'strangers have always been excluded, and rightly so' (Jelinek 2004 [1997]: 50, 54). At the same time, Jelinek also detects *anthropophagic* demands for assimilation, which she appears similarly committed to opposing: near the beginning of the play, one of its anonymous characters thus declares with insincere, feigned compassion: 'you four poor things, who made the mistake of not taking on the appearance and the name of our acquaintances in time' (Kosta 2003: 95).

The terrible circumstances that triggered Jelinek's play remove it somewhat from the realm of the everyday. There are, however, also more regular, routine and, in part, institutionalized forms of cultural pluralism which position themselves in critical opposition to both *anthropoemic* strategies and *anthropophagic* expectations. I have argued elsewhere that such critical and inclusive discourses are articulated by parts of the local press in Austria's two main cities: criticisms of the exclusions suffered by asylum seekers across 'Fortress Europe' as well as a celebration of ethnic diversity and multi-dimensional, culturally hybrid identities are thus articulated by, for example, a weekly Viennese newspaper and a monthly street magazine published in the south-eastern city of Graz (Karner 2007). Another relevant example illustrates that cultural pluralism need not be confined to the realm of civil society and political commentary. In the spirit of 'inter-cultural learning' and in light of a sizeable local Turkish community, the training for future primary schoolteachers in the western region of Vorarlberg now includes compulsory Turkish language courses (http://vorarlberg.orf.at, 30 November 2005): clearly, the relationship between ethnic majorities and cultural 'others' need not be based on permanent exclusions or on inevitable one-way assimilation; 'self' and 'other' can jointly create spaces of dialogue, mutually enriching interaction and cultural hybridity.

The everyday: its politics, its politicization

I argued in Chapter 1 that, along with historically variable contexts, two social dimensions are key to understanding everyday life: first, issues of power and possible resistance as enacted, experienced and endured by individuals and groups in the course of their day-to-day routines and biographies; second, the issue of reflexivity or its absence, which raises the question whether or not people think about the conditions of possibility underpinning – as well as about the consequences to – their everyday lives. In what follows, we briefly examine instances of everyday life challenging the very distinction between self and other upon which both *anthropoemic* and *anthropophagic* responses to the stranger are based. We thus encounter the counter-hegemonic potential of everyday life: practices, ideas and lives defined by cultural hybridity challenge – intentionally or otherwise – rigid ethno-national boundaries. As such, the cultural ambivalence of the everyday subverts nationalist discourses encountered not only in Austria but also across and beyond 'Fortress Europe'. On the basis of select and illuminating discursive snapshots I distinguish between two forms of such counter-hegemonic everyday lives: on the one hand, the inherent *politics of the everyday*, which is 'merely' lived and not articulated consciously; and, on the other hand, the reflexive *politicization of everyday life*, which draws attention to cultural syncretism and ethnic diversity in order to intentionally deconstruct and challenge nationalist discourses of identity and belonging.

A revealing example of the *politics of everyday life* (see also Karner 2005b) has been recorded in the southern province of Carinthia, a region with a history of territorial conflicts with neighbouring (now former) Yugoslavia. In recent years, memories of these conflicts have been revived by disputes over (additional) bilingual topographic road signs – between in numerical terms increasingly marginal parts of the German-speaking majority (e.g. Lackner 2006: 13) and sections of the Slovenian-speaking minority; the regional government currently headed by Jörg Haider appears, at the time of writing (spring 2006), reluctant to provide some bilingual topographic signs in parts of the province, despite relevant clauses in the state treaty of 1955, a recent ruling by the country's highest court and widespread public and political criticism. It is thus against a historical backdrop of ethnic/territorial conflict – but crucially also in the context of cultural syncretism, bilingual institutions and everyday lives lived by many at the intersection of traditions and languages – that the following instance of the *politics of the everyday* must be understood. The instance in question is recorded by another representative of what we might term Austria's contemporary critical literature – the author Peter Turrini: it involved Turrini sitting in a local pub and conversing in Slovenian with a fellow writer, when they found themselves verbally attacked by a local farmer. The latter, Turrini recalls (2001: 68–69), declared that this was 'German-speaking territory' on which there was no space for the Slovenian language; to Turrini's amusement, the farmer had got so agitated that he failed to realize that he himself had slipped into Slovenian. In terms of our current discussion, Turrini's recollections are highly relevant for two reasons. First, they illustrate that the rigid boundaries and categories constructed by discourses of ethnic/national identity and belonging are not infrequently crossed and thereby challenged by the ambiguities of everyday life, by culturally hybrid or in this case bilingual life histories. Second, this instance raises the issue of reflexivity and its absence: while Turrini is acutely conscious of the contradiction between the farmer's *espoused* (nationalist) ideology and his *lived* bilingualism, the farmer himself appears not to be. It is in this sense that we may understand the non-reflexive *politics of the everyday*: the seemingly most mundane of activities and taken-for-granted of practices, such as the speaking of languages, are inflected by configurations of power and hence often shaped by histories of conflict and exclusion. In other words, everyday life is always lived in wider contexts of inequality, difference, boundaries and hierarchies; the everyday is inherently political, even though some or all of its political dimensions may elude our awareness some or all of the time.

This stands in contrast to the reflexive *politicization of everyday life*, whereby its political characteristics are brought to the forefront of public consciousness and debate. Particularly relevant to our present discussion are attempts to raise more widespread consciousness of the type of contradiction recorded by Turrini, to draw attention to how the everyday refuses to conform to the rigidity demanded by ethno-nationalist ideology.

An example of the active politicization of cultural hybridity, formulated as a deliberate challenge to ethnic exclusion, was provided by a collection of biographical essays (Coudenhove-Kalergi 2001) published in the aftermath of the above-mentioned and controversial inclusion of the Austrian Freedom Party in a coalition government in February 2000. Reflecting on their respective lives and family histories, the various contributors to this collection of essays – artists, intellectuals and politicians – collectively problematized the very notion of a culturally homogeneous 'national identity'; they did this by recording and celebrating the social realities of ethnic exogamy (i.e. inter-ethnic marriage), cultural syncretism, and the creative mobilization of different and co-existing 'traditions' by individuals and their families. A series of reflections on the everyday experience of cultural diversity, the essays combined biographical glimpses with political statements aimed at deconstructing primordial and exclusive conceptualizations of Austrian national identity. These counter-hegemonic accounts thus also provided insights into biographies that are in popular discourse frequently represented as 'hyphenated identities', whether Jewish-Austrian, Slovenian-speaking Austrian, South-Tyrolean or Austro-Croatian. Such hyphenation, some of the contributors revealed, is in itself a partial distortion, since it suggests an over-simplified compartmentalization of everyday lives that are shaped by bi-/multilingualism and interlocking ethnic traditions. In other words, rather than being easily disentangled, different languages and cultural traditions are constantly being negotiated and often creatively merged by the social actors in question. Culturally hybrid life histories must of course also be seen in their wider contexts of power, inequality and exclusion. The idea that national identities are culturally monolithic and the privileged possession of an ethnic majority found its most explicit challenge in the editor's declaration (Coudenhove-Kalergi 2001: 8, my translation) that 'there is no typically Austrian identity, not even one of diversity. There are only identities. Every life-history is different.'

Not dissimilarly, another contributor (and formerly high-ranking politician) observed that 'positioning' somebody's identity is a near-impossible task, since people are inevitably the product of a diversity of cultural currents and histories (Busek 2001: 20). This line of critique was developed further by a Green Party politician, whose challenge against exclusivist discourses of national belonging resembled Stuart Hall's re-conceptualization of identities as ongoing 'routes of becoming' rather than the 'roots of being' they are widely but misleadingly assumed to be: 'Humans do not have roots, we are not trees. But they imagine that they have roots. We may all do that [to some extent]' (Stoisits 2001: 96; my translation). This particular example of counter-hegemony is therefore premised on the observation that in the context of the everyday, cultural boundaries are inevitably blurred, constantly crossed and negotiated. Against the backdrop of the growing mobilizing power of neo-nationalism, the collection of essays discussed here epitomized a particular form of political challenge: its reflexive engagement with the intricacies of the everyday led it to observe and argue that lived social realities and actual biographies contradict and subvert – in their cultural complexities and ambivalences – the artificial rigidity of the boundaries drawn by nationalist discourses. In other words, cultural hybridity was being politicized in order to challenge the exclusion of the 'stranger' from the self-defined ethnic majority and to question their very distinction.

Questioning boundaries, challenging exclusion

The second half of this chapter has drawn attention to select examples of critical discourse that variously challenge rigidly exclusivist ideologies of national identity as well as, more widely, the structural exclusion of groups of 'strangers' from and within 'Fortress Europe'. While I have not addressed the question as to how widely articulated, how representative and influential these discourses are, our discussion makes a sociologically crucial point: it shows that ethno-national communities are social constructs, that the boundaries delineating them from groups of 'others' are subject to ideological contestation and therefore potential historical change. As we have seen, such discursive struggles over mechanisms and structures of exclusion often occur – in Austria as elsewhere – in the realm of cultural production. The above examples of opposition to both *anthropoemic* strategies of exclusion and to *anthropophagic* mechanisms of assimilation have fallen into two categories: first, discourses of cultural pluralism, which celebrate and seek to preserve ethnic diversity; and, second, critical reflections, which suggest that culturally hybrid life histories and everyday practices challenge the very opposition between an ethnic self and others.

As a final step to the analysis undertaken in this chapter, I would like to briefly draw attention to another discursive snapshot, which combines (albeit in inverse order) these two strategies of counter-hegemony: a contribution to Austrian popular music (see also Karner 2002) – a reflexively political song entitled 'I bin aus Österreich' (STS 2000), translated as 'I am from Austria'. The song in question positions itself, right from the outset, in the realm of political critique levelled against discourses of national belonging and exclusion: translated somewhat loosely, the song begins by stating that 'recently, all this "blood, soil and people" nonsense is becoming fashionable again, I really don't want to hear it'. From there on, the lyrics examine what they portray and celebrate as Austria's inherent cultural diversity: the song thus paints a picture of the singer's own (fictitious or actual) family history shaped by grandparents who were variously German-speaking mountain farmers, ethnic Hungarians and Roma; the result is a form of cultural hybridity embodied by individuals, which consequently challenges attempts at 'clear' group classification and boundary maintenance. In other words, the song celebrates individuals' 'mixed' family histories and self-identifications, which are partly traced to the history of the multi-ethnic Habsburg empire and make ethnic hybridity the rule rather than the exception. In terms of the current discussion, parts of 'I bin aus Österreich' thus amount to a deconstruction of rigid self–other distinctions grounded in the historical and everyday realities of ethnic intermarriage, cultural diffusion and syncretism as well as their embodiment by individuals. The song subsequently and subtly shifts in its portrayal of Austrian society by presenting a picture of a multicultural mosaic of ethnic communities. In other words, having detected hybridity within individuals' biographies, the song then celebrates cultural pluralism, locates difference on an aggregate group level and implicitly advocates the protection of such group diversity against both *anthropoemic* exclusion and *anthropophagic* assimilation. The lyrics therefore also include lines – intended to capture ethnic diversity (through multiple voices) in contemporary Austria – to the effect of 'I am from India, I am a Palestinian . . . I am a young Roman, I am an elderly Croatian, it would be a great loss if it was any different'. Combining the two critical discursive strategies examined above, the celebration of (everyday) hybridity and cultural pluralism respectively, the song's political message seems clear: the nationalist exclusion of (presumed) ethnic others is historically/sociologically as untenable as it is ethically bankrupt.

CONCLUSION

In this chapter I have focused on various contemporary Austrian conceptualizations of ethnic/national sameness and otherness. Zygmunt Bauman's argument about the necessary complementarity and parallel application of *anthropoemic* and *anthropophagic* strategies, with the former advocating the stranger's exclusion and the latter demanding their assimilation, provided the conceptual starting point to our discussion. Drawing on relevant survey findings, public discourses and policies, the first part of our analysis indeed confirmed the co-existence, in contemporary Austria, of such exclusivist and assimilationist strategies respectively. However, I went on to demonstrate that dominant ethno-national identities are in certain contexts also conceptualized in hierarchical fashion, based on assumed degrees of relative similarity and difference between the national self and various (ethnic) others. I then turned to contemporary civil society and select contributions to Austrian cultural production in order to reveal alternative responses to 'the stranger'. Appropriating Antonio Gramsci's terminology, I referred to such alternative discourses as counter-hegemonic strategies that problematize, challenge and subvert the discursive/institutional exclusion, marginalization or demanded assimilation of strangers not only in Austria but also across 'Fortress Europe'. I discerned two distinctive strategies of such counter-hegemony – the celebration of ethnic diversity and of culturally hybrid biographies/everyday lives respectively.

This analysis has emphasized that discursive struggles over the ethnic majority's responses to the stranger need to be seen in context: in Austria, the significance of history – particularly World War II and the Holocaust – to debates about self–other relationships has been shown to be of the utmost significance. Moreover, I have argued that the recently renewed appeal of neo-nationalist discourses – those being based on rigidly *anthropoemic* exclusions while also at times articulating strong *anthropophagic* demands – needs to be understood in the context of rapid social change and profound political and economic transformations. In other words, contemporary globalization provides the wider and crucial context to the competing discourses examined in this chapter: both exclusivist ideas about national belonging and attempts to create inclusive, multi-ethnic, transnational civil societies constitute reactions, albeit diametrically opposed ones, to a period of far-reaching structural change (Karner 2005a, 2007). Furthermore, I have shown that the everyday is a crucial site and resource for such competing reactions to perceived contemporary crises. To illuminate this further, I have distinguished between the non-reflexive *politics of everyday life* and the reflexive *politicization of the everyday* respectively: the former captures the fact that seemingly self-evident ideas can have histories of conflict and exclusion and that taken-for-granted cultural practices may inadvertently subvert consciously articulated political preferences; the *politicization of everyday life*, by contrast, aims to bring the cultural complexities and ambivalences of the quotidian to the forefront of public consciousness and debate.

It should be noted once again that, due to constraints of space, I have said relatively little about the relative representativeness of these competing discourses and their various definitions of the self–other relationship: the main objective in this chapter has been to record their co-existence and hence to draw attention to discursive struggles within a dominant ethnic majority, to show that social boundaries are contested and to cast some light on the significance of everyday life to such struggles.

While contemporary Austria of course needs to be understood in the context of its own history, it also offers insights and lessons of much wider relevance. Crucially, the construction of boundaries by ethnic majorities and the exclusions experienced by groups of 'strangers' are highly topical issues all across and far beyond 'Fortress Europe'. Moreover, the articulation of critical discourses in the realm of civil society and the politics of cultural production are by no means peculiarly Austrian phenomena. In addition, the impact of globalization is felt across the world, and the reactions to its promises, perceived opportunities, costs, risks and dislocations appear to be as varied in many other parts of the globe as they are in Austria. Finally, my observations pertaining to the everyday also possess considerably more general significance: they raise questions about the role of cultural hybridity and of reflexivity or its absence in the contexts of our everyday lives. In broad conceptual terms, then, this chapter has shown that dominant *structures of action* and *ways of seeing* encountered among an ethnic majority are subject to considerable internal debate, ideological contestation and potential historical transformations.

In the next and final chapter, we will examine questions of ethnicity and everyday life as experienced by majorities *and* groups of 'strangers' in the context of one of today's most heatedly debated topics – forced migration and asylum. In doing so, we will re-encounter many of the themes we have addressed thus far, while putting particular emphasis on two of the dimensions discussed in Chapter 1: first, the important argument that everyday lives are profoundly shaped by changing historical contexts; and second, the observation that ethnicity also furnishes *structures of feeling*, both among dominant majorities and numerical minorities.

5

FORCED MIGRATION AND *STRUCTURES OF FEAR* IN THE AGE OF GLOBALIZATION

The main themes we have discussed through our case studies in the three previous chapters have included the following: the exercise of power on ethnic groups by various means of social classification, control, and exclusion; the everyday as a potential site of group identification and/or resistance; the continuous negotiation of (ethnic) identities in the context of multiple structures of power and inequality; cultural hybridity and the everyday; discursive struggles among ethnic majorities over group boundaries and their permeability for 'strangers'. Each of these themes has a bearing on our final case study, which centres on experiences surrounding one of the most widely and heatedly debated contemporary issues – forced migration. In slight contrast to the two previous chapters, I will replace a clearly delineated geographical focus with a more widely cast empirical net; although many of the studies I draw on are UK-/EU-based, a global framework (see e.g. Castles 2003) is crucial to understanding the reasons behind forced migration as well as some of the reactions among 'host populations' in the countries where refuge is sought. More accurately, we will see that forced migration and the very often disconcertingly hostile reactions to asylum seekers – arguably the epitome of 'the stranger' or the person who comes today and, seeking protection, hopes to stay tomorrow – need to be analysed as symptoms of contemporary globalization.

In terms of our theoretical framework (and while continuing to emphasize the centrality of power and the role of reflexivity), the focus of our discussion therefore now shifts to the effects of changing historical contexts on everyday lives. We will also encounter further illustrations of *structures of action* and *ways of seeing* being subject to debate, contestation and potential transformation, among dominant majorities as well as among the marginalized and disenfranchised. Moreover, we now also turn to the third dimension of ethnicity emphasized earlier: its provision of *structures of feeling*. I argue that in the contemporary world these are significantly shaped by uncertainty, anxiety and fear, both among ethnic majorities and excluded strangers (though of course in very different ways and for vastly different reasons).

Following a brief overview of the history of migration to Europe since the end of World War II, I provide a summary of seminal sociological analyses of the contemporary era and of (economic) globalization as arguably its defining characteristic. I also examine briefly the complexity of factors triggering forced migration in our rapidly globalizing world and, in the process, question some of the bureaucratic categories and discursive distinctions frequently applied to people who variously escape from armed conflict, political persecution, environmental degradation and economic hopelessness. Tracing forced migrants from some of their countries of origin through their hazardous journeys to their frequently hostile reception in, or rejection from, relatively more privileged parts of the world, we will examine the place and significance of ethnicity in their everyday lives at each of these stages. Later parts of the analysis move the focus from 'the stranger' back to dominant ethnic majorities, whose heterogeneous reactions are interpreted as contrasting responses to a world of risk and anxiety, perceived instability and insecurity. It must be stressed at the outset that constraints of space merely allow for a discussion of very specific examples of truly global and highly complex phenomena: these examples have been chosen because they offer important insights into everyday ethnicities in the context of one of today's most pressing issues.

HISTORY, GLOBALIZATION, OFFICIAL CATEGORIES

Tracing understandings and policies of asylum from antiquity to modernity, Liza Schuster challenges two common assumptions informing contemporary debates about asylum seekers and refugees: first, the idea that liberal democracies have a 'long and honourable tradition of granting asylum' and, second, the presumption that over recent years such institutional benevolence has been increasingly exploited by those commonly labelled as 'bogus asylum seekers' or 'mere economic migrants'. Schuster challenges these assumptions by showing that asylum pre-dates liberal democracy 'by millennia' (rather than vice versa) and by arguing that 'the exploitation has usually been carried out by states, including liberal democracies, whose asylum practice has always reflected state interest and only incidentally benefited individuals' (Schuster 2002: 40). Clearly, in order to engage with the suggestion that (economic) self-interest rather than humanitarian altruism has underpinned most immigration and asylum policy, we need to consider relevant literature on the recent history of migration (also see Bloch 2002). I thus begin by following Kate Reed's lead (2005) in tracing important similarities – such as the experience of social exclusion and everyday racism – and differences between contemporary asylum seekers and previous migrants to Western Europe. This raises important issues about the particularities of the contemporary era, about the local effects of economic globalization, about concomitant political transformations and the psychological implications of living in a fast-changing, risk-prone, conflict-ridden and highly unequal world. Relevant sociological theories of globalization and analyses of forced migration in turn raise important critical questions about the (in)accuracy of official categories and of commonly drawn distinctions, including that between 'economic migrants' and political refugees (e.g. Castles 2003: 17).

Post-war migration

Stephen Castles' summary of the history of migration to Western Europe in the post-World War II era provides a compelling illustration of how economic concerns and strategies have played a determining role in the channelling, organization and subsequent curtailment of mass migration. Post-war reconstruction followed by economic growth and increasingly widespread affluence relied on additional and cheap labour, a crucial economic requirement that the European industrial nations met either by encouraging mass-scale immigration from their (former) colonies or through 'guest worker' schemes:

> By the 1960s, migrant labour had become a structural feature of Western European labour markets. Abundant labour with low social costs was a vital factor in the long boom. This paved the way for subsequent family reunion and permanent settlement that was to lead to the multi-cultural Europe we know today.
>
> (Castles 2000: 7)

Multicultural societies in contemporary Europe are thus, to some extent, the unintended side effects of labour recruitment strategies in the three decades following the end of World War II. As Castles goes on to show (2000: 9–12), however, the end of the economic boom marked by the oil crisis of 1973 also soon translated into considerably more restrictive immigration and employment legislation. At the same time, the 1970s and 1980s were defined by a series of far-reaching, enduring and truly global economic transformations: the beginnings of the 'electronic revolution' and the transnational integration of financial markets (see also Castells 1996), the emergence of newly powerful economies on the Asian-Pacific rim (as well as new migrant flows to oil-producing countries and the Asian 'tiger economies') at the same time as economic downturns, job insecurity and the erosion of welfare states came to define the lives of many in Western societies; arguably most crucial was the growing ability and tendency of multinational corporations to move their investments from the 'high-wage economies of the old industrial heartland to low-wage export zones in the Third World' (Castles 2000: 9).

The period since the 1970s has also seen a sharp increase in a different type of migration – that embarked upon by asylum seekers who cross international borders and claim (very often unsuccessfully) refugee status as defined by the 1951 UN Convention Relating to Refugees: people who because of 'a well-founded fear' of persecution 'for reasons of race, religion . . . membership of a particular social group, or political opinion' are outside their country of nationality and are 'unable to or, owing to such fear, unwilling to avail [themselves] of the protection of that country' (quoted in Moorehead 2005: 28). The dramatic increase in the numbers of people seeking the protection of a state other than their own over the past three decades and the rarely mentioned fact that the majority of refugees never reach Western Europe but remain stranded near their country of origin are captured by the following statistics:

> The number of people seeking asylum in Western Europe, from what is now called the Third World, and more recently from the former Soviet Union and Eastern Europe, has increased from a few thousand a year in the early 1970s to nearly half a million per year now. . . . However, according to figures from the United Nations High Commission for Refugees (UNHCR), out of the 21 million refugees in the world as a whole only around a tenth are in Western Europe.
>
> (Hayter 2003: 8)

It must further be noted that a large proportion of people immediately affected by, for example, armed conflict or natural disasters never cross international borders but suffer as 'internally displaced persons' (IDPs). Moreover, mention must of course also be made of the much-discussed phenomenon of 'smugglers' illegally trafficking some of the most desperate of migrants along highly treacherous routes (e.g. Moorehead 2005: 30) and often under conditions of extreme exploitation and 'bonded labour' (e.g. Jordan and Düvell 2003: 101).

This briefest of summaries raises the central questions addressed in this chapter: *What do ethnicity and everyday life entail in the context of such changing migratory patterns and the profound economic transformations mentioned above? What triggers forced migration? How might we account for the often worryingly hostile reactions among the relatively affluent towards those escaping violence and/or economic destitution?* Put another way, we are interested here in the historical context and structural reasons underpinning contemporary forced migration.

Furthermore, important questions need to be asked about the different 'parts' played by ethnicity in variously contributing to migration flows and in providing a much-needed safety net for many asylum seekers and refugees. Crucially, those of us living in comparatively prosperous, politically stable and privileged parts of the world are confronted on a near daily basis with a discourse based on suspicion towards, rather than sympathy for, asylum seekers: how can this be? Are not compassion and solidarity the obvious response to such people, many of whom have escaped persecution or poverty and continue to experience racism in their everyday lives, who endure exclusions and uncertainty while awaiting decisions that – if they go against them – can mean deportation and hence further trauma, fear and often despair? Yet asylum seekers find themselves – in much public discourse – constructed as a 'drain on society', and 'rather than [us] capitalising on [their] skills and celebrating the cultural diversity they bring', they are turned into scapegoats (Reed 2005: 88–89). Can sociology aid our understanding of this without providing convenient excuses for widespread indifference and hostility? To at least begin a discussion of these complex and hugely important questions, we now turn to some seminal analyses of globalization and its effects.

The sociology of globalization

The literature on globalization is vast and constantly growing. In what follows, I thus confine myself to a very brief discussion of three influential sociologists, whose complementary theories provide particularly revealing vantage points with regard to the issues examined in this chapter. The three sociologists in question are Manuel Castells, Ulrich Beck and Zygmunt Bauman and their respective analyses, only highly select parts of which can be summarized here, go a considerable way towards illuminating the above-mentioned economic and political changes that have transformed the world since the 1970s.

In his trilogy on *The Information Age*, Manuel Castells argues that over the past three decades a new and truly global social formation has come about: a *network society* powered by information and communication technology, which transcends the boundaries of any one nation state and has created a 'space of flows' and exchanges between the economically dominant areas, or 'nodes', in various parts of the globe. As Castells also points out, however, this new global network of economic activity and communication is less inclusive than widely assumed: those areas excluded from the global space of flows – whether inner city ghettos in what used to be thought of as the 'first world' or huge areas of entire continents such as large parts of sub-Saharan Africa – suffer a truly debilitating form of social exclusion. Put another way, social and economic activities have been fundamentally altered by the rise of multinational corporations, the transnational integration of financial markets and the digital revolution; the resultant network society spans the world's financial centres and key economic actors, it is a world of instant communication, compulsory entrepreneurialism and flexibility, which – given the rigidities inherent in central planning – also partly explains the demise of communism; it is a world that is now beyond the control of governments, and where inequalities are becoming more pronounced and chronic. Crucially, however, the exclusions from the information age (or often the mere fear of potential future exclusion) endured by countless millions also breed various forms of 'resistance identities', among which Castells lists religious fundamentalisms and ethno-nationalisms, and which serve as vehicles of protest and as sources of meaning and solidarity in an uncertain and steeply hierarchical world.

The German sociologist Ulrich Beck continues to be associated with his hugely influential *Risk Society* (1992), first written in the aftermath of the nuclear disaster in Chernobyl in 1986. Beck observed that contemporary life had become defined by hazards and risks, which were truly global in their implications (rather than produced and experienced in self-contained localities) and the full extent of which even experts and their knowledge systems were at a loss to accurately estimate or combat. More recently, Beck (2000) has shifted his attention to the political implications of economic globalization including what he terms the contemporary 'denationalization shock': the ability of multinational corporations to strategically relocate to parts of the world where labour is cheap puts nation states into a constant state of competition for economic investment. Low taxes become a near necessity for attracting capital, and hugely important sources of tax revenue are therefore either lost altogether or substantially reduced. In any case, welfare states become increasingly difficult to sustain, a political development enacted by governments but ultimately driven by multinational business (and arguably the real locus of power). When confronted by 'chronic unemployment', which is endured by successive generations and highly unlikely to disappear with the next economic upturn, individuals can find themselves relatively abandoned by the political safety nets of yesteryear; in Ulrich Beck's words, people are left having to find 'biographical solutions of systemic contradictions' (1992: 137).

Several of these themes are further explored in Zygmunt Bauman's recent analyses (1998, 2000, 2004, 2005) of contemporary poverty, work and consumerism, social exclusion and migration – in short, of what he identifies as some of the *human consequences of globalization*. These include, according to Bauman, a new disjunction between global capital that has become 'nomadic' (and thus largely uncontrollable) and political institutions and everyday lives that continue to be tied to specific localities respectively. These consequences also include a new distinction between two types of strangers: on the one hand, wealthy tourists and the powerful global business elite who are received with open arms and cross borders with ease; on the other hand, the outcasts of *liquid modernity*, groups of 'vagabonds', the disempowered and persecuted, the marginalized and chronically excluded, among them asylum seekers who find themselves vilified, detained, dispersed or deported. Moreover, Bauman points out that contemporary polarizations are also experienced in relatively stable and comparatively affluent parts of the world – between thoroughly individualized consumers (who relate to each other and the world as commodities) and the new 'underclass', the excluded, permanently unemployed and local poor, so-called 'flawed consumers'. Even among those currently employed and thus able to consume and conform, however, fear of an uncertain future, the spectre of possible redundancy, 'vague and diffuse "security fears"' (Bauman 2005: 93) have become part of everyday life. All of this poses the question as to how people cope with chronic anxiety and, more accurately, whether discourses of belonging and hence exclusion are a reaction to such uncertainty and atomization.

Thus we arrive at a portrayal of the world at the beginning of the twenty-first century, which is as recognizable as it is disconcerting: a world of *both* economic integration *and* exacerbated polarizations and inequalities, a world of previously unknown risks, where real power arguably lies – in the final analysis – with multinational corporations whose strategic investments and relocations affect politics and local lives across the globe; a world of migration flows triggered by, as we shall see, diverse factors including political upheaval and persecution, environmental degradation and stifling poverty; but also a world in which far-reaching social transformations impact on individuals' psyches, creating a climate of chronic insecurity, to which discourses of ethnic, national or religious identity proclaim to offer some form of antidote. Before examining the role of ethnicity and everyday life under such historical/structural circumstances, the argument that contemporary forced migration needs to be understood in the context of globalization requires further discussion. In the process, questions pertaining to a common typology of migrants will arise.

Forced migration: reasons and categories

Adding to the above-cited figures, Stephen Castles quotes the following UNHCR statistics in support of his insistence that forced migration can only be understood against the backdrop of global social transformations and as an 'integral part' of contemporary North–South relationships: between 1975 and 1985 the global refugee population grew from 2.4 million to 10.5 million, and to 14.9 million in 1990; following a 'peak' of 18.2 million in 1993 (when, after the end of the Cold War, refugee flows particularly from war-torn parts of the previously communist Eastern bloc were at their strongest), it had declined to 12.1 million by 2000. However, this relative decline captures merely 'officially recognized refugees under the . . . 1951 UN Refugee Convention, which refers only to people forced to leave their countries due to individual persecution on specific grounds'; moreover, it needs to be seen in the context of the '"non-arrival regime" set up by developed countries . . . [leading] to the containment of refugees in their areas of origin'; this was partly reflected in the dramatic increase in internally displaced persons from 1.2 million in 1982 to 14 million by 1986 and to over 20 million by 1997 (Castles 2003: 14). The suggestion that refugee flows 'slowed down' between 1993 and 2000 is similarly qualified by Anthony Richmond, who points out that at the end of 2000, and counting 'returned refugees, the internally displaced and others of concern to the UNHCR', there were '21.8 million people in refugee or similar crisis situation, with Third World countries bearing the greatest burden' (2002: 719). Such figures clearly show that the era of globalization since the 1970s, with all its above-mentioned characteristics, has coincided with a dramatic increase in the numbers of asylum seekers and IDPs. The question remains, however, as to whether this has merely been a historical accident or, conversely, whether globalization creates structural conditions 'conducive' to forced migration.

To remind ourselves that we live in a world of profound inequalities is to state the insultingly obvious; to further observe that such inequalities reflect historically embedded power structures, social relationships of hierarchy and exclusion, systems of production, exchange, distribution and consumption that favour some and disadvantage many others is also an articulation of common knowledge. What is less widely acknowledged, however, is that inequalities have been exacerbated over recent decades (e.g. Storper 2001). The suggestion that in a global free market economy 'the rich are bound to get richer, and the poor relatively poorer' (Richmond 2002: 715) is worryingly corroborated by figures indicating that today 800 million people are 'permanently undernourished' and some four billion, 'two thirds of the world's population, live in poverty' (Bauman 2005: 84). Given that the majority of refugees flee civil wars and ethnic conflicts (e.g. Jordan and Düvell 2003: 66), the question then arises whether stark inequalities in an age of global transformations and ethnic conflicts are somehow interrelated. While we must certainly be very wary of simplistic, mono-causal explanations, it should also be remembered that ethnic networks have been observed to provide mechanisms of political mobilization and economic solidarity in contexts of crisis and intense competition over scarce resources:

> [E]thnic conflicts . . . have already killed millions. . . . The most intense conflict is likely to occur when rapid economic, political, social and

environmental changes occur simultaneously, as is the case in many parts of Africa, the Middle East and Asia today. The very speed of these transitions generates a high degree of insecurity and fear. Considering the rise of forced migration in sub-Saharan Africa, Findley . . . notes that the *'root causes of armed conflicts are often economic, involving a struggle to gain control over limited, precious economic resources.* Countries with dismal and deteriorating economic situations, rising unemployment, rampant inflation, and declining living standards are particularly at risk for political chaos, complex emergencies and forced migration.'

(Richmond 2002: 721; emphasis added)

The suggestion being made here echoes the instrumentalist interpretation of ethnicity, which holds that ethnic group membership provides a political asset in conditions of social inequality and economic scarcity, a way of competing more effectively for power and resources that utilizes existing social relationships of extended kinship, reciprocity, mutual support and obligation. Translated into our conceptual terms, ethnic *structures of action* can enable more effective competition for often extremely scarce resources; in the process, they reproduce cultural boundaries and may be used to exclude ethnic others. It must of course also be remembered that countless victims of ethnic violence-cum-asylum seekers originate from parts of the world with a history of colonial subjugation and, following decolonization, chronic political and economic instability. In other words, the historical roots of many contemporary conflicts leading to forced migration undoubtedly predate current global economic transformations. That said, however, the sociology of globalization summarized above indicates very strongly that in today's world profound and 'rapid economic, political, social and environmental changes' – the very prerequisites for ethnic conflict and forced migration highlighted by Richmond – are firmly in place.

To make sense of the dramatic increase in forced migration in the contemporary period, then, the following points made by Castles (2003: 16–18) need to be remembered: first, globalization has exacerbated inequalities, with 'trade, investment and intellectual property regimes that favour the industrialized countries [and] maintain underdevelopment in the South'; second, 'failed economies generally also mean weak states, predatory ruling cliques and human rights abuses'; and while many conflicts triggering forced migration can be traced to the era of colonialism and decolonization, their scale and intensity have often escalated since the 1980s – the early heyday of contemporary globalization. If we add to this the above-mentioned potential for ethnicity to be utilized as a political tool in conditions of scarcity, a highly volatile 'mix' of economic inequality and poverty, competition, the possibility of violent conflict and forced migration can be the outcome.

If forced migration triggered by ethnic conflict can frequently not be divorced from competition over scarce resources (and which in turn can often be counted among the local consequences of globalization), how tenable is the common 'Northern' typology that claims to unambiguously differentiate political refugees from so-called economic migrants? Two slightly different lines of argument may be discerned in the literature: on the one hand, the insistence that people fleeing political persecution, actual or likely violence, torture, rape or murder not only need special protection but that their experiences must not be conflated with other migrants'; Alice Bloch articulates this passionately by emphasizing that 'refugees do not choose to migrate but are forced to leave their homeland', making their lives and positions 'qualitatively different from [those] of voluntary migrants' (2002: 79). On the other hand, and while Bloch's reminder is a hugely important one, it has also been queried if the category of 'voluntary migrants' adequately captures the highly constrained or forced 'choices' made by many of the people labelled thus. In this context mention should be made of Caroline Moorehead's research on people crossing the border illegally between Mexico and California, which raises difficult questions about the meaning of the distinction between economic migrants and asylum seekers among people 'driven to the margins by need' (2005: 67). Similarly, Liz Fekete points out that particularly in the 'era of a globalized economy, where more and more people are displaced by war or by economic or environmental devastation . . . the distinction between an "economic refugee" and a "political refugee" is razor thin' (2005: 66–67). Stephen Castles provides the following examples of forced migration that can indeed be extremely difficult to classify:

Millions of people are displaced every year by development projects such as dams, airports, roads, luxury housing, conservation areas and game parks. . . . Typically, it is rural dwellers, ethnic minorities and indigenous people who suffer 'in the national interest', while elites and transnational companies benefit. . . . In addition, many people have to migrate because of environmental degradation, natural disasters and industrial accidents or pollution. In such cases, it is extremely hard to distinguish environmental, economic and political factors, so that the label 'environmental refugee' is misleading and even damaging, since it can divert attention from complex causes.

(Castles 2003: 15)

Let me be clear: none of these arguments challenges the special protection that political refugees need and should be given. What they do, however, is to query some of the connotations widely evoked by other groups of 'strangers' commonly (as well as often pejoratively) labelled as 'voluntary' or 'economic migrants'. Informed by the aforementioned sociology of globalization, we may ask some pertinent questions about a range of contemporary factors that can force people into migration: these include the local consequences and unequal distribution of environmental risks and health hazards, ethnic conflicts triggered by competition over scarce resources, and sheer economic hopelessness brought about by the stifling exclusion from the 'space of flows' of our highly unequal *network society*. In adopting a global perspective, we contextualize forced migration and we may begin to critically interrogate bureaucratic and popular typologies which ignore the fact that so-called economic migration also has political causes and can only be understood as a symptom of profound as well as often widening inequalities. Anthony Richmond (2002: 708–709) captures these complexities and nuances in arguing that 'there is no clear-cut distinction between "proactive" and "reactive" migrants, rather a continuum between those who have some freedom of choice . . . and those who are impelled by circumstances beyond their control. . . . Political, economic and social factors combine to propel and expel people.'

ETHNICITY IN FORCED MIGRANTS' EVERYDAY LIVES

Condensing parts of the argument presented in the previous section, existing classifications and bureaucratic typologies of migrants are sociologically less revealing than a broad category of *forced migration*. Such a critically re-conceptualized notion needs to subsume people escaping various forms of suffering: from political persecution and ethnic violence to environmental degradation and economic destitution, all of which can very frequently only be understood in the context of contemporary globalization, its inequalities, transformations, dislocations and risks. Put another way, the compulsion to migrate can have complex, varied and interrelated reasons, which the much-used distinction between political refugees and so-called 'voluntary economic migrants' often fails to capture. Moreover, rather than helping to allocate individuals to bureaucratically predetermined categories, sociological analysis should strive to illuminate the reasons – both structural/historical and specifically idiosyncratic – underpinning forced migration as well as the experiences of those forced to migrate. With regard to the focus of this book, we thus now address the following question: What, if anything, does ethnicity mean in the everyday lives of some such forced migrants prior to migration or at the point of their departure, and – after their often extremely hazardous journeys – during their uncertain stays or following settlement among often inhospitable host societies? Clearly, questions such as these tend to have context-specific answers. In what follows, I therefore largely confine myself to a discussion of select examples taken from very specific contexts. That said, the possibility of some careful generalization should be kept open: for example, when observing the 'use' of ethnicity for some asylum seekers in particular parts of 'Fortress Europe', we should certainly feel justified and encouraged to look for parallels and differences elsewhere.

Everyday cultures of hoped-for migration

An example of such context-specific insights is provided by Tarik Sabry's study (2005) of everyday symbols and rituals surrounding actual or desired emigration from Morocco. Migration to Europe, either with the help of hard-to-obtain visas or as undocumented migrants, is for many among the urban unemployed of Casablanca the only potential way out of their positions of hardship and chronic marginalization. In this context, Sabry investigates the centrality of hoped-for emigration in three cultural realms: everyday talk about migration in densely-populated working-class areas; popular jokes; and the physical space, practices and interactions in the queues outside Western embassies. Among these, Sabry's ethnographic observations conducted in the queues outside the Italian and French embassies are particularly relevant for our current purposes: they provide insights into some of the meanings and manifestations of everyday ethnicity at an institutional site where the gatekeepers of 'Fortress Europe' and some of those hoping to gain access to it meet.

The queues outside Western embassies, Sabry argues, constitute contradictory, 'dual cultural spaces', in which the powerful external bureaucracies of Western modernity intersect with the queuers' 'world'; the latter 'accommodates . . . non-institutionalized cultural particularities that are inherently Moroccan' (Sabry 2005: 15). In other words, the queues – and the everyday practices of those hoping, often in vain, to obtain a visa to a Western country – are about power and resistance, about shared ethnicity, about human agency and the attempt to overcome structural disadvantages and exclusions. At the very site where external powers and those attempting to transcend their current exclusion come face to face, Sabry observes everyday 'camaraderie' among Moroccan queuers; while the outside world provides some hope to those living with unemployment and hardship, their more immediate experience of that outside world – as encountered at the gates of its embassies – is 'bureaucratic and alienating'; yet, in the face of uncertainty, bureaucratic hurdles, confusion and likely frustration, the queuers liberally share information, food, jokes, cigarettes, and discuss their prospects of obtaining a visa, their chances of finding a job in Europe, and the likelihood of experiencing racism upon arrival. In short, 'the world of the queuers manages, in its entrapment and confusion, to be both intimate and sociable' (Sabry 2005: 16).

Sabry's ethnographic observations among some of the generally 'unheard and unseen' also map on to our earlier conceptualization of ethnicity and everyday life: passports, visas, embassies, queues, likely rejections and possible migration are all manifestations of the *structures of action* provided by ethnicity and citizenship, which either enable or constrain certain decisions and courses of action for those variously included or excluded. Put another way, the implications of being Moroccan and hence holding a non-EU passport act as partial determinants of what is or is not possible, or at least likely, for the people who Sabry observes. Moreover, the queues outside Western embassies in Casablanca provide a compelling illustration of the everyday being shaped by (institutional) power and inequality. At the same time, however, Sabry's observations of sociability and intimacy among Moroccans queuing outside embassies may be interpreted as an example of what De Certeau (1984) terms the everyday *tactics* employed by the weak and marginalized in order to temporarily evade power or, at the very least, cope with their own positions of (relative) powerlessness.

While being Moroccan and the hope for a better life abroad are the obvious common denominators among the queuers, Sabry also provides glimpses of ethnic distinctions and diversity among them:

> 'I won't get your dossier until you tell me where you come from,' demanded Said, teasing an old peasant wearing a traditional Moroccan *Jellaba*. ... There was a long pause and then the peasant, looking sheepishly at Said, uttered: 'Ben Meskin.' This made everyone fall about laughing. ('Ben Meskin' is a Moroccan *Aroubi* tribe notorious for emigrants who generally make their money in Italy selling carpets and watches on beaches or in the street.) Said, too, burst out laughing, slapped the old man's head then held it with his two hands and kissed it violently. ... [Then] he held the old man's hand and said: 'Now, I'll go and fetch your dossier.' Said, and perhaps all the people in the queue, had known exactly where the old man had come from. His clothes were a giveaway. It was the confirmation they enjoyed.
>
> (Sabry 2005: 18)

Clearly, in the queues outside these Western embassies, the main power differential and ethnic boundary are those separating local Moroccans from powerful European outsiders. That said, Sabry here also provides glimpses of internal cultural differences among

Moroccan queuers: these are here reflected in clothes as boundary markers and in local stereotypes of the people wearing them (which those making fun of the old man and he himself are clearly aware of). As discussed in Chapter 2, everyday ethnicity once again turns out to be crucially shaped by external power, while simultaneously being structured along lines of internal difference and providing evidence of quotidian *tactics* – here those of humour and camaraderie – to cope with structures of inequality and situations of powerlessness.

War, dislocation, gendered *structures of feeling*

Barbara Franz's comparative research (2003) among a different group of forced migrants – Bosnian refugees in Austria and the USA respectively – provides numerous important insights. Among these, two are particularly relevant to our current discussion. First, Franz investigates experiences of forced migration under extremely different circumstances and at a later stage in the 'process' of escape, migration and resettlement; her informants had been granted 'temporary residence' status or were recognized 'convention refugees', who had fled the violence, murder, ethnic cleansing and warfare that had – to the world's horror – defined the disintegration of former Yugoslavia in the early 1990s. Second, Franz's findings inadvertently also capture the third dimension of ethnicity mentioned earlier: ethnicity as providing more or less widely shared *structures of feeling*, or (sub-)culturally specific 'thought[s] as felt and feeling[s] as thought' (Williams 1977: 132). As mentioned in Chapter 1, it is arguably in situations of crises – such as those experienced by many forced migrants/refugees – that the least tangible parts of previously taken-for-granted everyday cultures can become objects of reflection, mourning, debate and conscious self-definition as well as potential political mobilization.

The individuals who Franz interviewed in Vienna and New York City respectively had escaped war, violence and the disintegration of political structures and social relationships. In addition to the trauma of migration, loss and exile they were confronted with new structures of relative exclusion or expected assimilation, while having to come to terms with the fact that forced migration had also entailed drastic downward social mobility. In other words, for many Bosnian refugees the loss of social status added further to the pain and hardship of rebuilding their own and their family's lives under such extremely difficult circumstances. Crucially, however, Franz reveals considerable differences in men's and women's respective resilience, their apparent ability to start all over again, and the significance of cultural meaning and role expectations in their rather contrasting coping strategies: Bosnian refugee women are portrayed as forward-looking, focused on their children's education, relatively uninterested in the politics of nationalist exclusivism (that had played such a crucial role in their displacement), and committed to their culturally defined roles in the patriarchal family, whose socio-economic recovery in alien and adverse circumstances became their overriding aim; Bosnian refugee men, by contrast, were considerably more backward-looking, strongly affected by the loss of social status, prone to both nostalgia and ideologies of primordial belonging and ethnic exclusion. In other words, Franz's findings suggest that Bosnian refugees' *structures of feeling* were, to a significant extent, gender-specific:

> Male Bosnian refugees still struggle more than ... their female counterparts with ... loss of belonging and status, and the war that changed their lives forever. The men have more trouble accepting the exodus and status degradation than do women ... Muslim men frequently focused on ... their lost feeling of belonging. ... Ethnicity defined in a primordial sense, as an exclusivist marker based upon blood and land, frequently appeared in the men's narratives. ... Through their ... loss of social status and material possessions ... important social and ethnic boundary markers of men's identity disappeared. Because of this loss, many Bosnian men still felt paralyzed ... in a limbo ... They lived in a world of memories, idle talk, jokes, folkloristic references, and parables.
>
> (Franz 2003: 98)

This stands in considerable contrast to Bosnian refugee women, who appeared to find solace, inspiration and some direction in repertoires of cultural meaning and practice, which – though geographically transplanted – remained a salient part of their everyday lives and played a role in their attempts to make the best of very difficult situations:

[T]he women defined their Bosnian identity through cultural and religious traditions such as . . . methods of food preparation or, for Muslims, fasting during Ramadan. Thus, [they] understood their own ethnic identity as not . . . necessarily linked to a particular place, primordial ties, or even political categories. Based upon their own interpretation of the refugee situation and their construction of identity, which manifested through cultural and religious traditions and focuses on the family and children, Bosnian women . . . realized that they had to act pragmatically and . . . began rebuilding their future from the bottom of the economic ladder.

(Franz 2003: 101)

The gendered *structures of feeling* Franz reveals among Bosnian refugees are therefore defined by nostalgia and pragmatism respectively. While her male informants displayed a paralysing attachment to their previous social standing and a discourse of primordial belonging, the women were future-oriented and continued to define their own roles in relation to the family, their children's education and advancement.

In this context, it is also worth noting that Franz's study maps on to a theoretical lead explored in Chapter 1 – Pierre Bourdieu's suggestion (1977) that situations of crisis transform the previously taken-for-granted 'universe of the undiscussed' (or *doxa*) into a domain of competing opinions, contradictory discourses and reactions. I argued earlier that Bourdieu's model is highly relevant to a discussion of ethnicity and everyday life for three interrelated reasons: first, it provides an illuminating way of conceptualizing culture as 'undiscussed' everyday common sense; second, it draws attention to the transformative power of social crises, as a result of which the formerly taken-for-granted becomes the focus of reflection, interpretation, debate and disagreement; third, it locates ethnicity in this latter realm of discourse and politics and thus defines the difference between ethnicity and culture as one of reflexivity/ consciousness or their absence (see Vertovec 2000; Karner 2005a). Although Franz does not directly invoke Bourdieu, her empirical findings both validate and refine this model: they indeed corroborate that the far-reaching effects of social crises, as in this case experienced by Bosnian refugees, heavily impact on people's varying self-understanding, cultural practices and ideas, as well as on their reflexive engagement with their past, present and future lives. Moreover, Franz shows that – in the context of her study – gender correlates very significantly with contrasting discursive and emotional reactions to crisis.

Instrumental ethnicity

Existing research on asylum seekers and refugees also highlights the significance of another key theme in the study of ethnicity: as mentioned earlier, the instrumentalist interpretation of ethnicity is based on the observation that – in certain circumstances – group membership, cultural meaning, social networks of solidarity, mutual support and reciprocal obligations can provide important coping mechanisms, channels of mobilization and strategies of adaptation to an alien social environment.

Alice Bloch's book (2002) – based on research conducted in the London Borough of Newham – about asylum seekers and refugees from Somalia, Sri Lanka and the Democratic Republic of Congo identifies the following key factors shaping their diverse experiences of settlement and relative integration or marginalization: pre-migration characteristics including language skills and educational qualifications; gender and childcare responsibilities; length of residence; immigration status and its impact on (un)employment; and, crucially for our discussion in this section, 'the presence of an ethnic community [and] participation in community activities' (Bloch 2002: 2). While Bloch's research thus highlights individual-specific factors and emphasizes 'structural barriers' that negatively affect refugees' settlement, she also reveals the crucial function performed by ethnic networks and associations: these can help to mediate between individual refugees and their families on the one hand, and the host society as well as its state bureaucracies on the other. Bloch reports that newly arriving asylum seekers tended to, if possible, 'actively seek out people from their own communities and community organizations to help them with many of their needs in the early stages of settlement'; this had also resulted in tight-knit, geographically clustered social and kinship networks, which operated in the community language and often managed to provide much-needed advice and information as well as access to familiar foods and to community places of worship (Bloch 2002: 160–161). It was also predominantly such informal community networks that subsequently provided refugees with information about social security benefits and employment; furthermore, Bloch reports that ethnic networks often proved crucial to finding jobs. Moreover (and contrary to popular clichés), such tight ethnic communities did not prevent 'integration' or alienate people from their surrounding environment:

> [N]early all the Tamil respondents interviewed were involved in religious and/or cultural activities pertaining to their community and were the group most likely to see Britain as home and least likely to say that they would return home should the situation permit return migration.
>
> (Bloch 2002: 186)

The benefits of such cultural familiarity and networks of social support become even clearer when they are declining or absent, a possible 'side effect' of the much-debated policies of asylum seeker dispersal introduced by the 1999 Immigration and Asylum Act (see Bloch and Schuster 2005). While intended to alleviate the 'burden of provision' previously carried by London, Bloch predicts that dispersal policies will further marginalize asylum seekers and deprive them of some much-needed support networks and information channels, leading her to argue that 'dispersal should be reassessed' (2002: 195–196). Caroline Moorehead goes a step further in suggesting that not only can the 'politics of dispersal' inadvertently erode ethnic support structures but that, in the process, the social isolation and existential despair suffered by some asylum seekers may be intensified: reflecting on the tragic suicide of a Guinean asylum seeker in Newcastle on New Year's Day 2002, she thus wonders if the fear and loneliness commonly experienced by asylum seekers was in this case perhaps aggravated by the fact that his native language was Fula, which is spoken in parts of West Africa, and that 'there were no other known Fula speakers in the whole of north-east England' (Moorehead 2005: 129).

These and other empirical studies provide corroborating evidence for the general observation that ethnic group membership can be of particular significance in situations of hardship, uncertainty or struggle; that is, culturally shared meaning, pre-existing social relationships and ethnic loyalties can provide vital safety nets or mechanisms of mobilization. Stephen Castles therefore describes ethnic minority 'enclaves' as performing a crucial task of 'self-protection (in both material and psychological terms) against a hostile environment' (2000: 89). Caroline Moorehead's global 'journey among refugees' illustrates this instrumental aspect of ethnicity in various contexts. Particularly revealing and moving is her account of a group of young refugees from Sierra Leone and Liberia (many of them of Mandingo ethnic background) in Cairo, who barely manage to survive, and thanks only to the bonds between them:

> [H]aving lost his grandparents, parents, seven brothers and sisters, several aunts and uncles, and many cousins, [Donzo] fled to Cairo and . . . live[d] with eleven other young Africans . . . I started visiting them at home so that they could show me, with a mixture of pride and embarrassment, how they were coping. . . . In two high-ceilinged rooms . . . these eleven [sic] young men have two broken beds, two chairs, three blankets, a light-bulb and a very old, erratic television set. The glass in the windows up the staircase [is] broken. . . . Rubbish fills every corner and down the . . . stairs . . . trickles an open sewer. . . . It is almost completely dark. Donzo and his companions live on $40 a month, the allowance received from UNHCR by the one Sierra Leonean recognised as an official refugee. At the beginning of the month, when the money comes . . . they eat rice and some vegetables cooked in oil; by the end they are down to just bread.
>
> (Moorehead 2005: 9)

A group of young men who have escaped one of the many armed ethnic conflicts which – as pointed out earlier – can only be understood against the historical backdrop of the nineteenth and twentieth centuries and, more immediately, in the context of contemporary inequalities, exclusions and power struggles; a group of young men who, having escaped conflict and violence, continue to live in fear, poverty and uncertainty: might this be the darkest side of everyday ethnicity in our globalizing world? And yet, in the midst of destitution and despair, is Moorehead not also conveying the vital importance of ethnic solidarity as a last remaining foothold in a world that has largely forgotten about these 'lost boys of Cairo'?

The instrumental uses of ethnicity, or their necessity, can also be significantly shaped by the relationship between migrants and the state structures of their host societies. More accurately, the ways in which groups of migrants are thought of, conceptualized, classified and responded to can impact on the salience of their ethnic identities. In some cases, as shown by Lynette Kelly's research (2003) on Bosnian refugees in Britain, a dominant framework that takes migrants' cultural otherness and particularity for granted can make the *construction* of previously non-existing communities an opportune, rational choice.

If communities are defined as clearly delineated, close-knit social entities with shared values, collective goals and strong internal bonds of reciprocal obligations, Kelly argues that the Bosnian refugees who first arrived in the UK in the early 1990s did not constitute such communities. There are several reasons for this: though the majority of Bosnian refugees were Muslims, others were of Serbian, Croatian or mixed backgrounds; also, they were internally differentiated along regional, educational and economic/class lines. Moreover, while everyday lives prior to the disintegration of Yugoslavia were defined by close inter-communal links (as reflected in the high incidence of mixed marriages particularly in the cities), the scale and horror of the war in Bosnia replaced 'multireligious and multiethnic coexistence' with lasting distrust and a profound 'psychological separation'; at the same time, internal factionalism and rivalries also made the notion of a distinct, homogeneous Bosnian Muslim community less than plausible (Kelly 2003: 44–45). Crucially, however, the refugees who Kelly discusses now found themselves in a context where migrants tended to be classified in communal terms in line with the British version of multiculturalism: this model is premised on the assumption that individuals are defined – first and foremost – as members of self-contained cultural communities, it allocates important resources on that basis, and it has been criticized for consequently overlooking conflicts and diversities within assumed groups (e.g. Baumann 1999). In general terms, Kelly corroborates the above-mentioned observations that community associations can be of vital significance to migrants by providing information, material and psychological support, as well as a sense of cultural belonging in times of trauma, exile, loss and uncertainty. However, she also insists that the case of Bosnian community associations suggests that community formation, far from being inevitable, can be a response to surrounding political structures and their tacit bureaucratic expectations; some of the communities thus formed will be 'contingent', reliant on the efforts of certain individuals-cum-community leaders, a way of entering into 'dialogue with the state', of gaining public recognition and – crucially – access to 'financial and practical support' (Kelly 2003: 39–42). In other words, 'contingent communities' form as a rational response to the assumptions informing the host society's allocation of important resources, but they do not necessarily reflect people's (cultural) self-understanding:

> [Bosnian community associations are] contingent communities, whose existence is dependent on the continued efforts of a few individuals and the availability of funds which can only be accessed through a formal association. Rather than being a formal expression of an informal community, the associations are a formal construction of an ideal and do not reflect the reality of their members. . . . There are kinship groups, friends and networks, but there is no community and no feeling of obligation to [it]. The associations reflect the expectations of British society and as such, their continued existence is dependent upon . . . a continuing social policy focus on refugee communities.
>
> (Kelly 2003: 46)

Importantly, Kelly's findings shift the emphasis on to individual and collective agency and the way cultural repertoires and group boundaries are actively reshaped in order to cope, as well as possible, with extremely difficult circumstances and alien environments. In true instrumentalist fashion, cultural communities and identities turn out to be resources mobilized and/or fashioned in response to the demands, workings and ideas of the surrounding host society. On a more general level, Kelly also inadvertently corroborates a point made in the previous chapters: many ethnic identities are significantly shaped by the interactions between dominant outsiders and existing political structures on the one hand, and groups of 'strangers' struggling to overcome their structural disadvantages on the other. In this particular case, *culture* is the generally recognized 'currency' in the interactions between the powerful and the relatively powerless; as a consequence, the latter appropriate a particular discourse of culture that stands in some contradiction to their everyday realities but is recognized as the most promising strategy of accessing important resources.

The discussion presented in this section has contained a succession of snapshots of what everyday ethnicity means and entails for some forced migrants of particular backgrounds, at different points in the process of planned or actual migration, and hence in very particular locations and circumstances. As such, these snapshots must remain firmly contextualized and cannot be seen as representative of the experiences and lives of the many millions of people worldwide forced into migration by violence, persecution, environmental disasters, social exclusion, stifling poverty, or – quite frequently – a combination of these factors. However, the above examples do reveal some of the *possible* meanings, dimensions and 'uses' of everyday ethnicity in the context of forced migration: first, ethnicity as a major axis of inequality structuring people's lives, being lived and negotiated in the realm of the everyday; second, the trauma of loss, migration and exile and its potentially differential impact on ethnic *structures of feeling* as experienced by different individuals or segments within communities of (forced) migrants; third, ethnicity as a vital resource mobilized to deal with displacement, marginalization, as well as the rules and dynamics of unfamiliar social and political environments.

In the final section of this chapter, we return to ethnic majorities, to the comparatively powerful, safe and privileged. In asking questions about their widely (though certainly and luckily not invariably) hostile reactions to forced migrants, we will discover that many among such ethnic majorities perceive their relative privileges, if they enjoy any of those at all, to be under threat or erosion. Relevant sociological literature suggests that local 'panics' about asylum seekers also need to be understood as a symptom of contemporary globalization and its dislocations. The latter have arguably affected widespread *structures of feeling* among host societies, replacing confidence and direction with fear and anxiety.

'LIQUID MODERNITY', ETHNIC MAJORITIES, *STRUCTURES OF FEAR*

We saw in Chapter 4 that Georg Simmel's definition of 'the stranger', as the person 'who comes today and stays tomorrow', has provided the conceptual basis for recent analyses (e.g. Bauman 1993) of societal responses to cultural otherness, ranging from exclusion to enforced assimilation. Writing about refugees as a particular category of strangers (whose migration has been forced rather than voluntary), Emma Haddad argues that they personify a form of radical otherness: involuntarily displaced, refugees subvert the most fundamental premises of a world of nation states, or what Haddad terms the 'territorial basis to political life' (2002: 24). Put another way, in a system that equates states and citizenship with territory refugees find themselves occupying precarious 'no man's lands' between states and hence a position of non-belonging. To the territorially grounded and well-protected citizens of receiving states meanwhile, refugees represent an ambivalent anomaly. On the one hand, they act as 'imagined others' – or the 'constitutive outside' – that facilitate the formation of national identities; this is another way of saying that identity requires difference, that 'in-groups' can only define and recognize themselves through the differences they perceive in, or attribute to, 'out-groups'. On the other hand, refugees fall in between categories, belong neither here nor there: as a consequence, they are seen as a threat to an entire system of classification, its taken-for-granted boundaries and politics (Haddad 2002: 34).

In suggesting that refugees constitute 'points of reference' that are simultaneously needed and threatening to dominant national identities, Haddad's argument provides a useful starting point for an analysis of widespread hostility towards forced migrants. However, it does not account for the worrying fact that such sentiments seem to be on the increase. A comprehensive analysis of xenophobia as directed at forced migrants needs to be historically contextualized: it forces us to return to the above-mentioned sociology of globalization and of its political as well as psychological impact on local, everyday lives.

The contradictions of a globalizing world?

Analyses of globalization, migration and local reactions to (forced) migrants (see e.g. Grillo 2005) reflect a striking and disconcerting tension: on the one hand (and very worryingly), they reveal increasing hostility in comparatively rich, industrialized and now post-industrial countries towards some of the world's most chronically excluded and most violently persecuted. On the other hand, analysts of contemporary globalization have also pointed out that migration is more than a by-product of contemporary social transformations: it is also a requirement, perhaps nowhere more so than among affluent yet 'ageing populations'.

Paul Gilroy offers the following reflections on the contemporary state of affairs inside 'Fortress Europe':

> Europe stands today militarized once again and heavily fortified against its proliferating enemies, within and without. The war against asylum seekers, refugees, and economic migrants offers a chance to consider . . . changing patterns of governmentality, commerce, and labour [and] to examine the changing cultural and ethical contours of Europe, where . . . the practice of politics seems to be in irreversible decline – undone by a combination of consumer culture, privatization, and the neoliberal ideology.
>
> (Gilroy 2004: 155)

Others also observe that while the aforementioned 'war against asylum seekers' may be undeclared, it carries tremendous costs. Liz Fekete argues that Europe – driven by widespread xeno-racism, the populist media and 'target-setting' bureaucracies – has developed a 'deportation machine': designed to 'reduce the numbers of those seeking asylum, to raise the bar for successful claims and return those whose claims have "failed"', certain asylum and deportation policies threaten to undermine international conventions pertaining to refugees, to human rights and in some cases even to children's rights (Fekete 2005: 64). Jordan and Düvell made a similar argument two years earlier: they observed (2003: 145) that in some of the world's most prosperous countries asylum seekers, and hence some of the most vulnerable or chronically disadvantaged, are 'contained under conditions that would be abuses of civil and social rights' if they were applied to citizens of those countries.

Paraphrasing such extremely worrying analyses, we may indeed wonder if narrow targets concerning the processing of asylum applications and the rate of rejections now outweigh human rights concerns in some of the relatively privileged parts of a rapidly globalizing and highly unequal world. However, and as emphasized by Fekete (2005), it would be far too simplistic to lay the blame squarely on political actors who tend, after all, to at least partly respond to what they regard as public opinion and hence as a determinant of political success or failure. Indeed, even the briefest of glances at the tabloid press reveals the everyday pervasiveness of anti-asylum seeker sentiments. Put another way, we must entertain the possibility that this form of xenophobia is all around us, omnipresent, structural and that, inadvertently or otherwise, we are all to some extent part of it. It must be stressed that I am not suggesting that everyone agrees with such hostility towards some of the most marginalized and oppressed of people (thankfully they do not), but merely that simplistic allocations of blame will not do: this is not about particular political parties or individuals, though there are of course some that become the willing mouthpieces for such contemporary racism and exclusion. Instead, we need to think of anti-asylum-seeker sentiments as engrained in our recent history, in our political and social structures, the transformations they have been undergoing and, crucially, as related to some of the psychological consequences of contemporary globalization that were briefly mentioned earlier.

Widespread hostility towards forced migrants sits in stark contradiction to two other recurring themes in sociological analyses of contemporary migration: first, the fact that the numbers of people claiming asylum in comparatively rich yet increasingly 'fortified' countries have declined over recent years; second, the highly plausible argument that particularly the dominant nodes of the global *network society* require, if anything, more rather than less immigration.

According to UNHCR statistics, in 2004 the numbers of asylum seekers 'coming to the industrialized world' fell by 22 per cent compared to the previous year and to 'its lowest level since 1988' (www.unhcr.ch, 2 March 2005). However, this decrease barely registered with sections of the tabloid press whose headlines bemoaning a 'new asylum fiasco' and declaring that 'we've had enough' (Slack 2004; Slack and Little 2005) continued unabated. Soon thereafter a study by the Institute of Public Policy Research (IPPR) confirmed that asylum seekers were faced with 'deepening hostility' by sections of the media and the public; among the latter, the report suggested that hostility tended to be based on fear of competition for 'scarce local resources such as housing, healthcare and jobs' (quoted on http://newsbox.msn.co.uk, 30 June 2005). We will return to these seeming motivations underpinning anti-(forced) migrant sentiments in due course.

It is occasionally pointed out that some of the world's most affluent societies are also defined by ageing populations, the joint result of increasing life expectancies and declining birth rates that are indicative of the fact that parts of these populations have come to regard parenthood as a choice rather than a taken-for-granted part of the life-cycle (e.g. Dench *et al.* 2006: 114). Even without the above-mentioned difficulties surrounding the maintenance of costly welfare states in the globalization era (e.g. Bauman 1998; Beck 2000), such demographic developments raise serious questions about the future ability of states to provide health care and pensions for its (ageing) citizens. State provision, put very simply, relies on tax revenue, which in turn requires a sizeable and active labour force. One answer, and I would argue the only ethically acceptable answer, is to allow for more rather than less inward migration. In other words, it stands to reason (e.g. Richmond 2002: 712) that 'net inward movements of population' will become necessary to counteract the effects of low European birth rates, to 'avert population decline', and to ensure financial viability (on the aggregate, societal level). Even a more short-term view, however, links contemporary social transformations with the demand for more (rather than less) migration. This is essentially an argument about class hierarchies in the contemporary information or knowledge economy. The concentration of money and power in the nodes of the global *network society* has not only created new business elites of managers, professionals, IT experts and consultants, but has also increased demand for a variety of 'service work' (e.g. Castles 2000: 76) of the kind often only provided by migrants and, particularly, by migrant women. Migration and steep inequalities are fundamental to everyday life in the world's metropolises:

> Proactive economic migration is the lubricant that keeps the wheels of the global capitalist system turning. . . . '[G]lobal cities', such as London, New York, Tokyo and Toronto, attract both the highest and lowest income earners. Among the latter are the women from Third World countries recruited as housekeepers, nannies, practical nurses and office cleaners.
> (Richmond 2002: 714; emphasis in original)

In other words, migration to the geographical centres of our *information age* already appears to be a functional requirement for a global system of both interconnectedness and inequality. In light of this, the inevitable question arises why, on the level of public discourse, immigration is not embraced but, more often than not, vilified. The sociologically most meaningful way of approaching this is not by asking 'Why do politicians not state these facts on a regular basis?' but should centre on the following question: Why do people – meaning why do 'we' – not want to hear them? Anything else is tantamount to endowing politicians with too much agency, and 'ordinary people' with too little.

Anxiety among the relatively affluent and fearful

I have argued that *history* (and hence the constant possibility and experience of structural as well as cultural changes) is one of the key dimensions required to understand the everyday. Moreover, I have argued that the major 'properties' of ethnicity include its provision of *structures of feeling*. Initially defined by Williams (1977: 132) as meanings that are 'actively lived and felt' and as 'thought as felt and feeling as thought', I have proposed that such *structures of feeling* capture ethnicity's least tangible characteristics: shared moods, memories, perceptions and emotions; embodied ideas and practices; biographically grounded associations and meanings. Moreover (and following one of Pierre Bourdieu's many illuminating observations), I have suggested that this affective dimension to ethnicity is frequently articulated in the context of crises, when a previously taken-for-granted cultural common sense becomes the object of collective reflection, debate and possible mobilization. Implicit in this argument is the observation that *structures of feeling* need to be understood in historical context, since crisis experiences – such as those triggered by rapid and unusually far-reaching social change – occur at particular points in time. In this section, this part of our conceptual framework is used to cast *some* sociological light on contemporary xeno-racism (Fekete 2005) as directed at asylum seekers by disconcertingly many among the world's relatively more prosperous. It must be stressed, however, that explaining racism is a notoriously complex and contested endeavour, involving aspects as varied as the human psyche, structural/historical/cultural contexts, institutions, forms of discourse, as well as particular personality types. What follows, then, is not a comprehensive explanation but an attempt to illuminate only one particular facet of contemporary hostilities towards asylum seekers.

There are strong and disconcerting indications that the social, economic and political transformations associated with globalization have coincided not only with an increase in forced migration (see above) but also with a rise in anti-immigrant sentiments among host societies. To make sense of these developments, we need to return to Castells' account (1996, 1997, 1998) of the *information age*, Beck's analyses (1992, 2000) of risk, politics and biographies in today's globalizing world, and Bauman's insights (2000, 2001, 2005) into the various symptoms of *liquid modernity* that range from the creation of a new, permanently excluded urban 'underclass' to the commodification of human relationships and intimacy. Between them (and condensing their lengthy and complex analyses into a series of keywords), these seminal sociologists portray the contemporary world as follows: first, as dominated by global and nomadic capital, whose ability to move transnationally undermines local/national politics; second, as divided between, on the one hand, the relatively few rich and powerful, and, on the other, the majority of the world's population that lives either in stifling poverty or with a degree of more or less permanent insecurity and the fear of future social exclusion; third, living under such circumstances carries social and psychological costs (including increasing atomization and endemic anxiety), to which forms of collective meaning and identity – such as those associated with national, ethnic or religious communities – are perceived to offer some form of antidote (see also Karner and Aldridge 2004).

It is against the backdrop of such far-reaching, seemingly all-pervasive and ongoing structural transformations that what Stephen Castles terms the 'racisms of globalization' need to be understood: such racism, Castles observes (2000: 179–183), has grown since the late 1980s when the end of the Cold War 'coincided with a serious recession and with an increase in the entry of asylum seekers'. Globalization has thus been experienced, also among the comparatively secure in relatively prosperous parts of the world, as a 'series of crises' affecting the national economy, social relations, culture and identity; economic restructuring, changing investment patterns/locations, rising levels of unemployment and the gradual erosion of welfare states all combine to make political power appear 'fragmented and opaque', and to heighten local feelings of insecurity. In such contexts, many local people are wrongly seeing 'newcomers as the cause of the threatening changes', which gives rise to racism as an expression of 'group and personal identity in a situation of crisis' (Castles 2000: 181–183). Of course (and quite apart from the human tragedy and injustice of these reactions), such racism constitutes a fundamental misdiagnosis of the nature of the crises, mistaking effects for causes, and failing to recognize asylum seekers as further symptoms – and as often far more adversely affected fellow victims – of the profound transformations summarized above. However, the underlying point is that contemporary xeno-racism needs to be seen in a context where 'the nation state still tends to exclude the migrant Other from full membership, while . . . gradually losing its capacity to protect its citizens from globalizing forces' (Castles 2000: 25).

How, then, do the dislocations of globalization impact on the everyday lives and the *structures of feeling* of ethnic majorities? Following Zygmunt Bauman's wide-ranging analyses of *liquid modernity* (2000, 2001, 2003, 2005) we can discern anxiety, fear, uncertainty and feelings of powerlessness as extremely common yet individually endured emotional reactions to the contemporary world. The reasons are structural and cultural in character; they include both the effects of recent social transformations and the unintended consequences of widely shared values, ideas and practices: the dominance of 'nomadic' global capital has replaced yesteryear's job security with precarious employment and the possibility of employers deciding to 'downsize', close or relocate; at the same time, unemployment (a state of affairs once assumed to be temporary) has mutated into 'redundancy', a form of permanent social exclusion endured by the 'new poor' and unlikely to lift with the next economic upturn; as welfare states begin to erode and the public sphere of debate and active citizenship dwindles, those still employed fear that redundancy could strike at them next. At the same time, consumerism has become the main pastime, the dominant source of (perpetual) identity (re-)construction and a mechanism of social control; moreover, consumerism also colonizes people's psyches, their self-understanding and relationships: intimacy and love are expected to deliver instant gratification, the feared alternative being yet another form of redundancy. Work, love and life itself have, according to Bauman, all become 'liquid' – a state of affairs that haunts us and informs contemporary popular culture:

> What we all seem to fear . . . is abandonment, exclusion, being rejected. . . . We fear being left alone, helpless and hapless. Barred company, loving hearts and helping hands. We fear to be dumped – our turn for the scrapyard. What we miss most badly is the certainty that all that won't happen – not to us . . . *Big Brother*, *The Weakest Link*, *Survivor* or whatever . . . version of 'reality TV' . . . all tell us the same story: that no one except a few solitary winners is truly indispensable . . . that survival is the name of the game of human togetherness and that the ultimate stake of survival is outliving the others.
>
> (Bauman 2004: 128, 131)

Nation states, once the locus of most meaningful power, are themselves severely constrained by the rules and forces of globalization and are struggling to cope with the local consequences of 'globally produced problems'.

It is against this historically specific backdrop, Bauman suggests, that the current 'asylum hysteria' needs to be understood: many ordinary and fearful social actors feel further unsettled by allegedly ever-increasing numbers of forced migrants, whose arrival is understood to imply additional competition for already scarce resources and insecure employment (also see Dench *et al*. 2006: 223). Thus, Bauman argues, chronic trepidation brought about by global forces is deflected on to more tangible 'objects' – the 'aliens nearby' who become 'easy target[s] for unloading anxieties prompted by widespread fears of social redundancy'; at the same time, state powers – conscious of their position of relative dependency on global dynamics, shifts and configurations – use increasingly draconian asylum legislation to 'reassert their impaired and weakening authority' (Bauman 2004: 63–66; see also Bloch and Schuster 2005: 509). In the terms of our discussion, the effects of current migration flows on host societies therefore seem to be twofold: first, they add to widespread *structures of feeling*, or 'thoughts as felt and feelings as thought', among ethnic majorities that centre on anxieties over possible social exclusion – on the fear of losing out in the competition for increasingly scarce resources; second, while the institutions of the nation state are challenged by contemporary globalizing forces, tightening the *structures of action* defined by asylum and immigration legislation becomes a mechanism for retaining significant aspects of state authority. This latter point is corroborated by Cwerner's analysis (2004: 77) of recent legislative developments designed to 'deter would-be asylum seekers', to 'streamline administration and speed up the determination process'. This new 'politics of speed', Cwerner argues, constitutes a way of maintaining a 'last bastion of perceived sovereignty (through the control of population movements)' at the very time when the multiple, complex and global migration flows of our contemporary era are widely perceived to subvert the power and borders of nation states. However, the unintended and somewhat paradoxical consequences of tougher asylum legislation also include the above-mentioned, much-discussed and 'fast-growing international market in the smuggling and trafficking of migrants across borders' (Cwerner 2004: 84, 77). The dilemma, it seems, revolves around a series of contradictions between the global and the local (also see Castles 2000: 128). While hugely consequential economic processes occur in the realm of the former, everyday lives – with their struggles and anxieties – continue to be lived in specific localities: it is there that the 'human consequences' (Bauman 1998) of globalization materialize; it is there that group boundaries are defined, asserted and negotiated; it is in specific localities in both the central nodes and the chronically excluded parts of our global *network society* that inequalities – the structural roots of which go to the heart of the *information age* (Castells 1996) – are endured, that injustices are suffered, dreams of a better life are dreamt, and fears of deteriorating fortunes spread.

Alternatives of solidarity

Lest it be assumed that *structures of anxiety-induced hostility towards strangers* are inevitable local reactions to the dislocations of globalization, this section briefly examines select alternative reactions of human compassion and solidarity. The arguments presented above suggest that anti-asylum-seeker sentiments are made more likely by the fact that life is widely perceived as precarious, employment and even human relationships as temporary and uncertain. Crucially, however, there is ample evidence of very different reactions towards forced migrants that make it impossible to 'excuse' hostility towards asylum seekers: these alternative reactions show that such hostility towards the other is never, and must never become, an inevitability; *structures of fear* may – particularly in our era of *liquid modernity* – be pervasive and plausible, but they do not short-circuit agency, our capacity for reflexivity, compassion and responsibility for each other. Such alternative reactions to a climate of crisis and uncertainty are not only possible, they are being lived by 'conscientious doctors, committed journalists and filmmakers, social workers, teachers, children's advocates, human rights campaigners' and various others who work with or for asylum seekers, or campaign for their human rights (Fekete 2005: 77).

Caroline Moorehead provides evidence of more impulsive acts of support and compassion that include the following: in September 2002 an attempt to smuggle a group of young Liberians on to European shores, crammed by traffickers onto a hopelessly overloaded vessel, ended in tragedy: shipwrecked off the southern coast of Sicily, at least thirty-five of the young Liberians drowned; ninety-five others were saved, thanks to the coastal police and the spontaneous help provided by local villagers. Over subsequent months, the latter continued to provide practical support for the survivors/asylum seekers in their midst, trying to arrange accommodation, sharing locally grown vegetables, providing clothes for and baptizing a new-born Liberian baby in the local church (Moorehead 2005: 49). In this case, local poverty and high unemployment did not stifle human compassion, with villagers transcending narrow self-interest and ethnic boundaries.

A not dissimilar example of solidarity between 'locals' and asylum seekers attracted considerable media attention in the summer of 2005. This was the case of a Malawian family of five – a mother and her four children – whose claims for asylum received much support from their local community in the Dorset town of Weymouth. The *Guardian* reported that the family had changed local attitudes towards asylum seekers to the extent that, when they were taken to a detention centre, a 'campaign to free the family was snowballing, spearheaded by the local churches and the children's schoolfriends . . . there was a candlelit vigil, a mass petition and a protest at parliament' (Olden and Harris 2005: 7). The family was released, given four months' leave to remain, but was eventually deported. The *Independent* subsequently reported a 'tearful goodbye' between the family and their local supporters, many of whom had 'fought tirelessly for six months to keep them in the country' (Judd 2005: 16).

Examples of inter-ethnic alliances, resistance to the exclusion of some forced migrants, and initiatives to raise public awareness of the suffering endured by some of the world's most marginalized and vilified could be multiplied. Such examples vividly illustrate both the politics of the everyday and – given the current topicality of the issue – its historicity. By way of a conclusion to this section, Cwerner's account of the insights and consciousness underpinning some such initiatives of compassion is worth quoting:

> Advocates of refugee rights tirelessly speak of the complex links, networks and histories that unite refugee-sending countries and countries of asylum. We are reminded of the links between poverty, oppression, colonialism and international trade. Beneath the surface of international and national legal instruments there lie a myriad of actions, past, present and future, that intertwine the fate of those who seek protection outside their countries of nationality with that of the receiving countries.
>
> (Cwerner 2004: 83)

Such alternative politics are thus informed by the realization that the contemporary world can only be understood in its totality, that its most pressing issues and most profound injustices involve us all, that exclusions based on narrowly drawn ethnic or national boundaries overlook our economic and political interconnectedness and ignore our arguably most fundamental ethical responsibility for the other. Moreover, such alternative politics emphasize that contemporary inequalities and migration flows have a longer history, in the course of which parts of humanity have enjoyed tremendous advantages and increasingly unsustainable luxuries. However, this has happened, albeit perhaps inadvertently when seen from the perspective of everyday life, at the expense – or at least to the exclusion – of the vast majority of the world's population.

CONCLUSION

This chapter has examined aspects of ethnicity and everyday life in the context of one of today's most heatedly debated issues – forced migration and asylum. The resulting discussion has drawn on the sociology of globalization, its economic transformations, political reconfigurations, social dislocations, environmental risks and psychological side effects. In terms of the conceptual framework guiding this book, this chapter has put particular emphasis on the historicity of the everyday and on the *structures of feeling* provided by ethnicity. Informed by a range of relevant studies, I have traced the significance of everyday ethnicity among forced migrants from their conflict-ridden and/or often hopelessly impoverished locations of 'departure' to their difficult and frequently failed attempts at a new beginning in relatively more secure and privileged parts of the world. In the process, I have focused on the potentially varied effects of crises on emotionally charged though previously taken-for-granted aspects of people's cultural *habitus*, as well as on the instrumental 'uses' of ethnicity as networks of solidarity, mechanisms of mobilization, and much-needed repertoires of shared meaning. This was followed by a discussion of the often disconcertingly hostile reactions towards forced migrants among the ethnic majorities of host societies: I argued that such anti-asylum-seeker sentiments are also indicative of particular *structures of feeling*, which are shaped by the anxieties typical of *liquid modernity*. I concluded with a brief discussion of alternative reactions of compassion for forced migrants; such alternatives illustrate that while structurally induced fears may make narrowly delineated solidarities plausible, they do not make them inevitable. Exclusions may be defensive reactions to situations of uncertainty and perceived crisis, but they seem impossible to reconcile with an ethics of universal human rights.

CONCLUSION

THE QUEST FOR INCLUSIVE MEANING

This book began by establishing conceptual frameworks for our two central ideas – ethnicity and everyday life. Ethnicity, I argued in agreement with recent explorations of Bourdieu-ian sociology (e.g. Vertovec 2000), may be thought of as 'politicized culture', culture conscious of itself. Put another way, in certain circumstances individuals may begin to reflect on their previously commonsensical cultural universe to subsequently draw on long-established ideas, practices and social relationships as a rationale for group mobilization. I further argued that we can do more than illuminate the relationship between taken-for-granted culture and self-conscious, politicized ethnicity: cultures/ethnicities furnish *ways of seeing*, *structures of action* and *structures of feeling* – taken for granted so long as they are 'merely' part of a *habitus*, and consciously articulated once culture turns into ethnicity. Crucially, however, I have repeatedly argued that while culture and ethnicity are deeply engrained in our biographies, capable of making life meaningful, an often necessary network of support and solidarity, and an important influence on many people's everyday lives, they are not – and should not be used as – convenient 'excuses'. We are frequently told that people do what they do because it is allegedly in their 'cultural make-up' to do so, because 'traditions dictate' thus, and because it is an expression of 'their identity' to do so. This book has consistently challenged such accounts, which are lazy and untenable: we are all endowed with agency; *ways of seeing, structures of action* and *structures of feeling* indeed inform, constrain and enable many of our practices, decisions and behaviours; they may seem glaringly obvious to us, and we tend to invest in them emotionally; yet they do not single-handedly determine who we are and what we do. People negotiate 'their' identities and cultural traditions. We are capable of reflection and resistance, of solidarity with the 'other' and of cultural innovation. In fact, whatever else culture is taken to be, 'it' – as argued by Williams and Bauman – includes *both* the traditional *and* the novel, it spans across *both* conformity *and* subversion.

It is in this respect that the everyday becomes crucial, as a site where power and possible resistance are experienced and enacted, where we may or may not think about who we are, about our present or desired place in the world, about group membership, about the 'good' or the 'right' way of living life. Moreover, the everyday is of course also the stage on which history is lived and performed. In other words (and as argued throughout this book), *power/resistance*, *reflexivity or its absence* and *changing historical contexts* provide the parameters, within which the everyday is lived and needs to be understood.

These frameworks informed our subsequent empirical case studies that were intended to illuminate various aspects of ethnicity and everyday life. The chapter on communities of Roma and 'Traveller-Gypsies' focused on issues of power and resistance. Informed by Richard Jenkins' (1997) distinction between 'social classification' and 'group identification', it examined some of the historically variable mechanisms and strategies of categorization, surveillance, control, assimilation, exploitation, marginalization, and, most infamously, genocide exercised on Travellers by powerful, sedentary outsiders. This was followed by a discussion of the everyday as a site of cultural resistance, in which various ideas and practices serve as important mechanisms of group identification and social reproduction. The chapter concluded with a discussion of the exercise of power and resistance *within* Traveller communities.

Chapter 3 focused on British South Asian (diaspora) communities. In conceptual terms, we continued our discussion of the workings and effects of power, while paying particular attention to the notion of 'identity'. Drawing on Stuart Hall, we examined British South

Asian identities as continually negotiated, multiply constrained by existing configurations of power and inequality, but as also involving agency-endowed individuals who are never completely or permanently defined – or *interpellated* – by any one discourse, power relationship or cultural practice. Particular attention was paid to the concepts of diaspora and hybridity: with the former emphasizing transnational connections and the latter drawing attention to the creative merging of culturally heterogeneous elements, the politics of everyday life revealed complexities not captured by popular discourses that demand or presuppose clear identities and mutually exclusive categories of belonging and exclusion.

In Chapter 4 we turned our attention to the internally contested relationship between dominant ethnic majorities and groups of 'strangers' (who were first defined by Georg Simmel as people who are seen to 'come today and stay tomorrow'). The case study used to illuminate this was contemporary Austria and the guiding theoretical thread was provided by Zygmunt Bauman's distinction (1993) between two co-existing societal responses to cultural otherness: first, *anthropoemic* strategies of separation/exclusion and, second, *anthropophagic* strategies of enforced assimilation. An examination of Austrian politics, civil society, cultural production and everyday life confirmed that these two strategies are indeed applied 'in parallel', but it also revealed other discourses based on alternative self–other relationships. These include ideas about relative (rather than absolute) national sameness/difference, as well as critical discourses that either celebrate cultural diversity and pluralism or question the very delineation of the ethnic/national self from various others. The realm of the everyday and its politics was shown to be crucial in this respect, as a social domain where self–other boundaries are frequently criss-crossed and thus negated, albeit sometimes merely inadvertently.

In our final chapter (Chapter 5) we examined the significance of everyday ethnicity among groups of forced migrants as well as among frequently hostile sections of 'Fortress Europe's' host populations. Theoretically, I argued that the sociology of contemporary globalization provides some vital insights into the factors triggering forced migration as well as into some very disconcerting reactions in some of the world's relatively more prosperous and safe areas. The affective dimension of ethnicity (captured by the notion of *structures of feeling*) and the instrumental 'uses' of group belonging were emphasized, as were the psychological symptoms – such as anxiety, uncertainty and perceived powerlessness – of *liquid modernity*.

While much ground has been covered, much more could be said – not least since the case studies presented in this book reflect its author's idiosyncratic interests and competence. However, I have attempted throughout to reveal the general in the particular: hence my insistence that ethnicity involves *structures of action*, *ways of seeing* and *structures of feeling*, and that understanding everyday life requires an engagement with *power/resistance*, *reflexivity (or its absence)* and *history*. As a conceptual framework this should – and, I hope, will – stimulate further debate and encourage applications in any number of empirical contexts not considered above. In this sense it also appears fitting to conclude by once more returning to what has arguably been the most important general theme – or subtext – underpinning this entire book. While everyday lives can only be understood in the context of several hugely important axes of power and inequality (e.g. Brah 1996) that include ethnicity, the everyday also provides constant evidence of another defining characteristic of human 'togetherness': agency – our above-mentioned capacity for reflection, resistance and the ability to act in contravention of cultural expectations or statistical probabilities. Such exercises of human agency are particularly revealing and important when they involve ethical choices that recognize the other's needs and, in the process, override self-interest. One of the most powerful illustrations of such other-directed agency was provided by a group of individuals now known as 'the Righteous among the Nations' (see Gilbert 2002): these were some 19,000 'ordinary citizens', since recognized and honoured by the Holocaust museum (*Yad Vashem*) in Jerusalem, who during World War II risked their own lives to hide or protect Jewish friends, neighbours or complete strangers from detection, deportation and almost certain murder at the hands of the genocidal machinery of Nazism. When, decades later, research on some of the Righteous was conducted, two particularly important facts came to light. First, the Righteous included individuals from every social position and walk of life (e.g. Weinzierl 1997) – clergy as well as soldiers, farmers as well as factory owners and workers, acquaintances as well as complete strangers to the people who they rescued, deeply religious individuals as well as agnostic humanists. Second, when asked for the reasons why they had taken such grave risks, strikingly similar answers were given time and time again (Gilbert 2002: 519–531): 'we did what we had to do', 'we did the only thing a decent person would do', 'I have done nothing other than any normal human being would have done', '[we] did what we thought had to be done – nothing more complicated'.

The extreme situations in which the Righteous found themselves and acted on only add to the importance and the irrefutability of the lessons they teach us: there can be no exemption from the ability to act with responsibility for the other, above and beyond calculated self-interest and possible costs. As such, the Righteous personify a responsibility we should all be able to recognize, albeit against our very different historical backdrop of the twenty-first century. Moreover, the Righteous act as a very painful reminder of how few of us ever live up to this most fundamental yet far too rarely enacted of human responsibilities: to recognize the needs and rights of our fellow human beings and to make their well-being – or in this case their very survival – a moral imperative that allows for no excuses or alternatives. Beyond teaching us this simultaneously most basic and most important of ethical lessons, the Righteous also condense several of the sociological themes that have accompanied us throughout this book: human agency, ideological opposition to existing power structures, the negotiability and contestation of dominant discourses of identity and exclusion, reflexivity, everyday life and its historical embeddedness.

Ethnicity, I have pointed out repeatedly in the preceding chapters, may be seen as a double-edged sword: on the one hand, in many contexts and to countless millions of people an invaluable source of meaning, direction, solidarity and support; and, on the other, a way of dividing the world, of drawing and maintaining boundaries, of distinguishing 'us' from 'them'. Crucially, the analyses presented in this book have emphasized that both dimensions can only be understood in their wider contexts. Both the apparent 'yearning' for community and solidarity (e.g. Bauman 1992) and the always political delineation of groups in opposition to outsiders have structural roots and therefore need to be analysed as part of their wider historical circumstances. Along with many of my academic colleagues, I am suspicious of attempts to sociologically predict the future (if for no other reason than – yet again – human agency, our ability to 'act otherwise' and hence to work critically towards the reconfiguration of entrenched social structures). That said, one prediction concerning ethnicity and everyday life seems so easy to make, it barely qualifies as a prediction but as a rather obvious reading of the signs of our times: perhaps the most elementary political and ecological challenge confronting us all, as a universal human collective, will be to create meaning and solidarity that are *inclusive* rather than exclusive. As human beings, we strive to create meaning, to explain the world and its mysteries to ourselves, to belong, to create places and groups we identify and associate with, to obtain answers to life's big questions. In light of Zygmunt Bauman's observation that ours is an era of global problems requiring global solutions, it seems obvious that this apparent need for a meaningful social world can no longer – or only at great peril – be based on group antagonisms, intolerance and exclusions; and even if narrow or short-term self-interest at others' expense was not to jeopardize future generations and the planet we share, the above-mentioned 'Righteous among the Nations' should be single-handedly sufficient to make an irrefutable ethical case for inclusive meaning and solidarity beyond us–them distinctions. In the terms used throughout this book, we surely must work towards *ways of seeing* that reconcile cultural specificities with a global perspective based on universal respect and responsibility for the other, every other. At the same time, history should have taught us that in the dynamics between (ethnic and other) *structures of action* and the individual, concern for the individual, every individual, their well-being, right and ability to fulfil their human potential and to make their own decisions, should override preoccupations with established ways of doing things; put another way, the thoughts, feelings and actions of individuals must surely be empowered, protected and enabled rather than silenced and predefined by the configurations of power in which they happen to find themselves.

Returning to my earlier and recurring point that both ethnicity and everyday life can only be understood in their wider historical contexts, let me conclude this book by raising a number of questions.

If Anthony Giddens (1991) is right in describing the contemporary 'late modern' era as a period of heightened reflexivity, are we being reflexive about the things that really matter, the things that really should concern us? Are we giving enough thought to the wider political contexts and consequences of our actions? Are we, for example, reflexive enough about the conditions of possibility and effects of our consumer practices? Are we at all reflexive about how we contribute, albeit inadvertently, to climate change and the widening inequalities between the many impoverished and the comparatively few rich and powerful? Are we concerned, perhaps with our next-door neighbours, about the economic uncertainties of a world dominated by global corporations? Do we think and worry about the uses of certain discourses of ethnic and national belonging that often emerge in such contexts? I have argued that everyday life is shaped by power/resistance, reflexivity or a lack thereof and changing historical contexts. Seen through this lens, how do our own everyday lives fare? Are we reflexive social actors, willing to interrogate our own positions in existing social relations and prepared to act if the rights of others are violated? Is this what a new sociology should perhaps strive to do – to turn analysis into criticism and encourage us all to take a (self-)critical stand in the world, a stand based on respect for the other, both individuals and groups? Is Zygmunt Bauman (1992, 2002) right in detecting a worrying erosion of the public sphere of citizenship, social critique and political debate? Is he right in arguing that 'consumerist seduction' is the primary means by which a new social (dis-)order of atomizing individualism and enormous inequalities of wealth and power is being perpetuated? If so, what can or should we do about it? Contemporary ethnicity and everyday life need to be approached and understood on the basis of such observations pertaining to their wider contexts. These questions should concern us all. There are no easy answers to any of them. They can only be raised here. They do concern us all.

REFERENCES

Abercrombie, N., Hill, S. and Turner, B.S. (1984) *Dictionary of Sociology*, London: Penguin.

Acton, T. (1974) *Gypsy Politics and Social Change*, London: Routledge & Kegan Paul.

Adunka, E. (2002) 'Antisemitismus in der Zweiten Republik', in H.P Wassermann (ed.) *Antisemitismus in sterreich nach 1945*, Innsbruck: Studienverlag.

Anderson, B. (1983) *Imagined Communities*, New York: Verso.

Anthias, F. (1998) 'Evaluating "diaspora": beyond ethnicity?', *Sociology*, 32 (3), 557–580.

—— (2001) 'The concept of "social division" and theorising social stratification: looking at ethnicity and class', *Sociology*, 35 (4), 835–854.

Arnaut, K. (2004) '"Out of the race": the poiesis of genocide in mass media discourses in Côte d'Ivoire', in G. Baumann and A. Gingrich (eds) *Grammars of Identity/Alterity: A Structural Approach*, Oxford: Berghahn.

Baert, P. (1998) *Social Theory in the Twentieth Century*, Cambridge: Polity Press.

Baldwin, J. and Mead, M. (1971) *A Rap on Race*, New York: Laurel.

Ballard, R. (1994a) 'Introduction: the emergence of Desh Pardesh', in R. Ballard (ed.) *Desh Pardesh: The South Asian Presence in Britain*, London: Hurst & Co.

—— (1994b) 'Differentiation and disjunction among the Sikhs', in R. Ballard (ed.) *Desh Pardesh: The South Asian Presence in Britain*, London: Hurst & Co.

Bancroft, A. (1999) '"Gypsies to the camps!": Exclusion and marginalisation of Roma in the Czech Republic', *Sociological Research Online*, 4 (3), available at http://www.socresonline.org.uk/4/3/bancroft.html.

—— (2005) *Roma and Gypsy-Travellers in Europe: Modernity, Race, Space and Exclusion*, Aldershot: Ashgate.

Barnes, B. (1975) 'Irish travelling people', in F. Rehfisch (ed.) *Gypsies, Tinkers and Other Travellers*, London: Academic Press.

Barth, F. (1969) 'Introduction', in F. Barth (ed.) *Ethnic Groups and Boundaries*, London: George Allen & Unwin.

—— (1975) 'The social organization of a pariah group in Norway', in F. Rehfisch (ed.) *Gypsies, Tinkers and Other Travellers*, London: Academic Press.

Bauman, Z. (1990) 'Modernity and ambivalence', in M. Featherstone (ed.) *Global Culture: Nationalism, Globalization and Modernity*, London: Sage.

—— (1992) *Intimations of Postmodernity*, London: Routledge.

—— (1993) *Postmodern Ethics*, Oxford: Blackwell.

—— (1998) *Globalization: The Human Consequences*, Cambridge: Polity Press.

—— (1999 [1973]) *Culture as Praxis*, London: Sage.

—— (2000) *Liquid Modernity*, Cambridge: Polity Press.

—— (2001) *The Individualized Society*, Cambridge: Polity Press.

—— (2002) *Society under Siege*, Cambridge: Polity Press.

—— (2003) *Liquid Love*, Cambridge: Polity Press.

—— (2004) *Wasted Lives: Modernity and its Outcasts*, Cambridge: Polity Press.

—— (2005) *Work, Consumerism and the New Poor* (2nd edn), Maidenhead: Open University Press.

Baumann, G. (1996) *Contesting Culture: Discourses of Identity in Multi-Ethnic London*, Cambridge: Cambridge University Press.

—— (1999) *The Multicultural Riddle*, London and New York: Routledge.

Baumann, G. and Gingrich, A. (eds) (2004) *Grammars of Identity/Alterity: A Structural Approach*, Oxford: Berghahn.

BBC 3 (2005) *Gypsy Wars*, 28 September.

Beck, U. (1992) *Risk Society*, London: Sage.

—— (2000) *What is Globalization?*, Cambridge: Polity Press.

Belton, B. (2005) *Questioning Gypsy Identity: Ethnic Narratives in Britain and America*, Walnut Creek: Altamira Press.

Berger, H.M. and Del Negro, G.P. (2004) *Identity and Everyday Life: Essays in the Study of Folklore, Music and Popular Culture*, Middletown, CT: Wesleyan University Press.

Berthoud, R., Modood, T. and Smith, P. (1997) 'Introduction', in T. Modood *et al.* (eds) *Ethnic Minorities in Britain: Diversity and Disadvantage*, London: Policy Studies Institute.

Bhachu, P. (2005) 'Diaspora politics through style: racialized and politicized fashion in global markets', in C. Alexander and C. Knowles (eds) *Making Race Matter: Bodies, Space & Identity*, Basingstoke: Palgrave Macmillan.

Billig, M. (1995) *Banal Nationalism*, London: Sage.

Bischof, G. (1993) 'Die Instrumentalisierung der Moskauer Erklärung nach dem Zweiten Weltkrieg', *Zeitgeschichte*, 20 (11), 345–366.

Bloch, A. (2002) *The Migration and Settlement of Refugees in Britain*, New York: Palgrave Macmillan.

Bloch, A. and Schuster, L. (2005) 'At the extremes of exclusion: deportation, detention and dispersal', *Ethnic and Racial Studies*, 28 (3), 491–512.

Botz, G. and Sprengnagel, G. (eds) (1994) *Kontroversen um sterreichs Zeitge-schichte: Verdr ngte Vergangenheit, sterreich-Identit t, Waldheim und die Hitoriker*, Frankfurt/New York: Campus Verlag.

Bourdieu, P. (1977) *Outline of a Theory of Practice*, Cambridge: Cambridge University Press.

Brah, A. (1996) *Cartographies of Diaspora: Contesting Identities*, London and New York: Routledge.

Brass, P. (1997) *Theft of an Idol*, Princeton, NJ: Princeton University Press.

Brown, M. (2000) 'Religion and economic activity in the South Asian popula-tion', *Ethnic and Racial Studies*, 23 (6), 1035–1061.

Brubaker, R., Loveman, M. and Stamatov, P. (2004) 'Ethnicity as cognition', *Theory and Society*, 33 (1), 31–64.

Bruckmüller, E. (1996 [1984]) *Nation sterreich: Kulturelles Bewußtsein und Gesellschaftlich—Politische Prozesse*, Vienna: Böhlau Verlag.

Busek, E. (2001) 'Abstammung allein kann es nicht sein', in B. Coudenhove-Kalergi (ed.) *Meine Wurzeln sind anderswo: sterreichische Identit ten*, Vienna: Czernin Verlag.

Camus, J-Y. (2002) 'Die radikale Rechte in Westeuropa', in W. Eismann (ed.) *Rechtspopulismus: sterreichische Krankheit oder Europ ische Normalit t?*, Vienna: Czernin Verlag.

Castells, M. (1996) *The Rise of the Network Society*, Oxford: Blackwell.

—— (1997) *The Power of Identity*, Oxford: Blackwell.

—— (1998) *End of Millennium*, Oxford: Blackwell.

Castles, S. (2000) *Ethnicity and Globalization: From Migrant Worker to Trans-national Citizen*, London: Sage.

—— (2003) 'Towards a sociology of forced migration and social transforma-tion', *Sociology*, 37 (1), 13–34.

Cohen, A. (1969) *Custom & Politics in Urban Africa: A Study of Hausa Migrants in Yoruba Towns*, London: Routledge & Kegan Paul.

Coudenhove-Kalergi, B. (ed.) (2001) *Meine Wurzeln sind anderswo: sterreichische Identit ten*, Vienna: Czernin Verlag.

Cwerner, S.B. (2004) 'Faster, faster and faster: the time politics of asylum in the UK', *Time & Society*, 13 (1), 71–88.

De Certeau, M. (1984) *The Practice of Everyday Life, Volume 1*, Berkeley: University of California Press.

De Certeau, M., Giard, L. and Mayol, P. (eds) (1998) *The Practice of Everyday Life, Volume 2*, Minneapolis: University of Minnesota Press.

De Cillia, R., Reisigl, M. and Wodak, R. (1999) 'The discursive construction of national identities', *Discourse and Society*, 10 (2), 149–173.

De Lange, N. (1986) *Judaism*, Oxford: Oxford University Press.

De Vos, G. and Romanucci-Ross, L. (1995) 'Ethnic identity: a psychocultural perspective', in L. Romanucci-Ross and G. De Vos (eds) *Ethnic Identity: Creation, Conflict and Accommodation*, Walnut Creek: Altamira Press.

Dench, G., Gavron, K. and Young, M. (2006) *The New East End: Kinship, Race and Conflict*, London: Profile Books.

Dwyer, R. (1994) 'Caste, religion and sect in Gujarat: followers of Vallabhacharya and Swaminarayan', in R. Ballard (ed.) *Desh Pardesh: The South Asian Presence in Britain*, London: Hurst & Co.

Eriksen, T.H. (1993) *Ethnicity and Nationalism: Anthropological Perspectives*, London: Pluto Press.

Essed, P. (1991) *Understanding Everyday Racism*, London: Sage.

Fairclough, N. (1992) *Discourse and Social Change*, Cambridge: Polity Press.

Fekete, L. (2005) 'The deportation machine: Europe, asylum and human rights', *Race & Class*, 47(1), 64–91.

Fenton, S. (2003) *Ethnicity*, Cambridge: Polity Press.

Foucault, M. (1991 [1975]) *Discipline and Punish*, London: Penguin.

—— (1998 [1976]) *The Will to Knowledge (The History of Sexuality, Volume 1)*, London: Penguin.

Frank, A. (2000) *The Diary of a Young Girl*, London: Penguin.

Franz, B. (2003) 'Bosnian refugee women in (re)settlement: gender relations and social mobility', *Feminist Review*, 73, 86–103.

Gardiner, M. E. (2000) *Critiques of Everyday Life*, London and New York: Routledge.

Garfinkel, H. (2004 [1967]) *Studies in Ethnomethodology*, Cambridge: Polity Press.

Geertz, C. (1973) *The Interpretation of Cultures*, New York: Basic Books.

Gellner, E. (1983) *Nations and Nationalism*, Oxford: Blackwell.

Giddens, A. (1984) *The Constitution of Society: Outline of the Theory of Structuration*, Cambridge: Polity Press.

—— (1991) *Modernity and Self-Identity*, Cambridge: Polity Press.

Gilbert, M. (2002) *The Righteous: The Unsung Heroes of the Holocaust*, London: Doubleday.

Gillespie, M. (1995) *Television, Ethnicity and Cultural Change*, London: Routledge.

Gilliland, M.K. (1995) 'Nationalism and ethnogenesis in former Yugoslavia', in L. Romanucci-Ross and G. De Vos (eds) *Ethnic Identity: Creation, Conflict and Accommodation*, Walnut Creek: Altamira Press.

Gilroy, P. (2004) *After Empire: Melancholia or Convivial Culture?*, Abingdon: Routledge.

Gmelch, G. (1975) 'The effect of economic change on Irish Traveller sex roles and marriage patterns', in F. Rehfisch (ed.) *Gypsies, Tinkers and Other Travellers*, London: Academic Press.

Goffman, E. (1990 [1959]) *The Presentation of Self in Everyday Life*, Harmondsworth: Penguin.

Grillo, R. (2005) '"Saltdean can't cope": protests against asylum-seekers in an English seaside suburb', *Ethnic and Racial Studies*, 28 (2), 235–260.

Guru, S. (2003) 'Transmission and transformation of Asian femininity in everyday life', *Everyday Cultures Working Papers*, 8, Milton Keynes: The Pavis Centre for Social and Cultural Research.

Haddad, E. (2002) 'The refugee: forging national identities', *Studies in Ethnicity and Nationalism*, 2 (2), 23–38.

Hainsworth, P. (2000) 'Introduction: The extreme right', in P. Hainsworth (ed.) *The Politics of the Extreme Right*, London and New York: Pinter.

Halfacree, K. (1996) 'Out of place in the country: Travellers and the "rural idyll"', *Antipode*, 28 (1), 42–72.

Hall, S. (1996) 'Introduction: Who needs identity?', in S. Hall and P. du Gay (eds) *Questions of Cultural Identity*, London: Sage.

Hancock, I. (1997) 'Duty and beauty, possession and truth', in T. Acton and G. Mundy (eds) *Romani Culture and Gypsy Identity*, Hatfield: University of Hertfordshire Press.

—— (2002) *We are the Romani People*, Hatfield: University of Hertfordshire Press.

Hanisch, E. (1994) *Der lange Schatten des Staates: sterreichische Gesellschafts-geschichte im 20. Jahrhundert*, Vienna: Ueberreuter.

Haslinger, J. (1995) *Politik der Gef hle*, Frankfurt: Fischer.

Häusermann Fábos, A. (2001) 'Embodying transition: FGC, displacement, and gender-making for Sudanese in Cairo', *Feminist Review*, 69, 90–110.

Hawes, D. and Perez, B. (1995) *The Gypsy and the State*, Bristol: SAUS Publications.

Hayter, T. (2003) 'No borders: the case against immigration controls', *Feminist Review*, 73, 6–18.

http://derstandard.at (2005) 'SPÖ will Reform des Staatsbürgerschaftsgesetzes nicht zustimmen', 26 September.

http://newsbox.msn.co.uk (2005) 'Asylum seekers face deepening hostility – study', 30 June.

http://vorarlberg.orf.at (2005) 'Volksschullehrer müssen Türkisch lernen', 30 November.

Hussain, Y. (2005) *Writing Diaspora: South Asian Women, Culture and Ethnicity*, Aldershot: Ashgate.

Hutchinson, J. and Smith, A.D. (1996) 'Introduction', in J. Hutchinson and A.D. Smith (eds) *Ethnicity*, Oxford: Oxford University Press.

Jelinek, E. (2004 [1997]) *Stecken, Stab und Stangl; Rastst tte; Wolken. Heim*, Reinbek: Rowohlt.

Jenkins, R. (1997) *Rethinking Ethnicity: Arguments and Explorations*, London: Sage.

—— (2002) 'Different societies? Different cultures? What *are* human collectivities?', in S. Malešević and M. Haugaard (eds) *Making Sense of Collectivity: Ethnicity, Nationalism and Globalisation*, London: Pluto Press.

Jordan, B. and Düvell, F. (2003) *Migration: The Boundaries of Equality and Justice*, Cambridge: Polity Press.

Judd, T. (2005) 'Hundreds protest as Malawian family are led away to be deported', *Independent*, 26 August, 16–17.

Karner, C. (2002) 'Austro-Pop since the 1980s: Two case studies of cultural critique and counter-hegemonic resistance', *Sociological Research Online*, 6 (4), available at http://socresonline.org.uk/6/4/karner.html.

—— (2004a) 'Between structure and agency: from the *langue* of Hindutva identity construction to the *parole* of lived experience', in G. Baumann and A. Gingrich (eds) *Grammars of Identity/Alterity: A Structural Approach*, Oxford: Berghahn.

—— (2004b) 'Theorising power and resistance among "Travellers"', *Social Semiotics*, 14 (3), 249–271.

—— (2005a) 'National *doxa*, crises and ideological contestation in contemporary Austria', *Nationalism and Ethnic Politics*, 11 (2), 221–263.

—— (2005b) 'The "Habsburg Dilemma" today: competing discourses of national identity in contemporary Austria', *National Identities*, 7 (4), 411–434.

—— (2007) 'Austrian counter-hegemony: critiquing ethnic exclusion and globalization', *Ethnicities*, 7(1).

Karner, C. and Aldridge, A. (2004) 'Theorizing religion in a globalizing world', *International Journal of Politics, Culture and Society*, 18 (1–2), 5–32.

Kaufmann, E.P. (ed.) (2004) *Rethinking Ethnicity: Majority Groups and Dominant Minorities*, London and New York: Routledge.

Kelly, L. (2003) 'Bosnian refugees in Britain: questioning community', *Sociology*, 37 (1), 35–49.

Kiddle, C. (1999) *Traveller Children: A Voice for Themselves*, London: Jessica Kingsley.

Kinnvall, C. (2002) 'Nationalism, religion and the search for chosen traumas: comparing Sikh and Hindu identity constructions', *Ethnicities*, 2 (1), 79–106.

Knowles, C. (1999) 'Race, identities and lives', *The Sociological Review*, 47 (1), 110–135.

Kosta, B. (2003) 'Murderous boundaries: nation, memory and Austria's fascist past in Elfriede Jelinek's *Stecken, Stab und Stangl*', in B. Kosta and H. Kraft (eds) *Writing Against Boundaries: Nationality, Ethnicity and Gender in the German-Speaking Context*, Amsterdam/New York: Rodopi.

Lackner, H. (2006) 'Haider allein zu Haus', *Profil*, 23, 13.

Lefebvre, H. (2002 [1971]) *Everyday Life in the Modern World*, London and New York: Continuum.

Lewis, G. (2004) 'Racialising culture is ordinary', in E.B. Silva and T. Bennett (eds) *Contemporary Culture and Everyday Life*, Durham: sociologypress.

Lewis, P. (1994) 'Being Muslim and being British: the dynamics of Islamic reconstruction in Bradford', in R. Ballard (ed.) *Desh Pardesh: The South Asian Presence in Britain*, London: Hurst & Co.

Mac Laughlin, J. (1999) 'Nation-building, social closure and anti-traveller racism in Ireland', *Sociology*, 33 (1), 129–151.

Malešević, S. (2002) 'Identity: conceptual, operational and historical critique', in S. Malešević and M. Haugaard (eds) *Making Sense of Collectivity: Ethnicity, Nationalism and Globalisation*, London: Pluto Press.

—— (2004) *The Sociology of Ethnicity*, London: Sage.

Mayer, V. and Koberg, R. (2006) *Elfriede Jelinek: Ein Portr t*, Reinbek: Rowohlt.

McCrone, D. (1998) *The Sociology of Nationalism*, London and New York: Routledge.

Modood, T., Besthoud, R., Lakey, J., Nazroo, J., Smith, P.,Vindee, S. and Beishon, S. (eds) (1997) *Ethnic Minorities in Britain: Diversity and Disadvantage*, London: Policy Studies Institute.

Moorehead, C. (2005) *Human Cargo: A Journey among Refugees*, London: Chatto & Windus.

Morgan, D. (2004) 'Everyday life and family practices', in E. B. Silva and T. Bennett (eds) *Contemporary Culture and Everyday Life*, Durham: sociologypress.

Okely, J. (1975) 'Gypsies travelling in Southern England', in F. Rehfisch (ed.) *Gypsies, Tinkers and Other Travellers*, London: Academic Press.

—— (1983) *The Traveller Gypsies*, Cambridge: Cambridge University Press.

Olden, M. and Harris, A. (2005), 'One last hope', *Guardian/G2*, 22 July, 6–7.

Orwell, G. (1962) *The Road to Wigan Pier*, London: Penguin.

Pelinka, A. (1990) *Zur sterreichischen Identit t: Zwischen Deutscher Vereinigung und Mitteleuropa*, Vienna: Ueberreuter.

—— (1998) *Austria: Out of the Shadow of the Past*, Boulder, CO: Westview Press.

—— (2000) 'Die rechte Versuchung', in H-H. Scharsach (ed.) *Haider — sterreich und die rechte Versuchung*, Reinbek: Rowohlt.

Pelinka, A. and Weinzierl, E. (eds) (1987) *Das Grosse Tabu: sterreichs Umgang mit seiner Vergangenheit*, Österreichische Staatsdruckerei: edition S.

Pick, H. (2000) *Guilty Victim: Austria from the Holocaust to Haider*, London/New York: I.B. Tauris.

Pogány, I. (2004) *The Roma Caf: Human Rights & the Plight of the Romani People*, London: Pluto Press.

Postert, C. (2004) 'Completing or competing? Contexts of Hmong selfing/othering in Laos', in G. Baumann and A. Gingrich (eds) *Grammars of Identity/Alterity: A Structural Approach*, Oxford: Berghahn.

Raj, D. S. (2000) '"Who the hell do you think you are?": promoting religious identity among young Hindus in Britain', *Ethnic and Racial Studies*, 23 (3), 535–558.

Ramji, H. (2005) 'Exploring intersections of employment and ethnicity amongst British Pakistani Young Men', *Sociological Research Online*, 10 (4), available at http://www.socresonline.org.uk/10/4/ramji.html.

Reed, K. (2005) 'Comparing new migration with old: exploring the issue of asylum and settlement', in C. Alexander and C. Knowles (eds) *Making Race Matter: Bodies, Space & Identity*, Basingstoke: Palgrave Macmillan.

Rehfisch, A. and Rehfisch, F. (1975) 'Scottish travellers and tinkers', in F. Rehfisch (ed.) *Gypsies, Tinkers and Other Travellers*, London: Academic Press.

Reisigl, M. and Wodak, R. (2001) *Discourse and Discrimination*, London and New York: Routledge.

Reiterer, A.F. (ed.) (1988) *Nation und Nationalbewußtsein in sterreich: Ergebnisse einer empirischen Untersuchung*, Vienna: VWGÖ.

Richmond, A. H. (2002) 'Globalization: implications for immigrants and refugees', *Ethnic and Racial Studies*, 25 (5), 707–727.

Sabry, T. (2005) 'Emigration as popular culture: the case of Morocco', *European Journal of Cultural Studies*, 8 (1), 5–22.

Sayer, A. (2002) 'What are you worth? Why class is an embarrassing subject', *Sociological Research Online* 7 (3), available at http://www.scoresonline.org uk/7/3/sayer.html.

Scheffel, D.Z. (2005) *Svinia in Black and White: Slovak Roma and their Neighbours*, Peterborough, Ontario: Broadview Press.

Schuster, L. (2002) 'Asylum and the lessons of history', *Race & Class*, 44 (2), 40–56.

Shaw, A. (1994) 'The Pakistani community in Oxford', in R. Ballard (ed.) *Desh Pardesh: The South Asian Presence in Britain*, London: Hurst & Co.

Shetty, P. (2005) 'Editor's letter', *Asiana*, 7, 5.

Sibley, A. (1981) *Outsiders in Urban Society*, Oxford: Blackwell.

Sibley, D. (1997) 'Endangering the sacred: nomads, youth cultures and the English countryside', in P. Cloke and J. Little (eds) *Contested Countryside Cultures*, London: Routledge.

Sillitoe, A. (1994 [1958]) *Saturday Night and Sunday Morning*, London: Flamingo.

Slack, J. (2004) 'Asylum: we've had enough', *Daily Express*, 15 November, 1, 4.

Slack, J. and Little, A. (2005), 'New asylum fiasco', *Daily Express*, 9 March, 1, 5.

Song, M. (2003) *Choosing Ethnic Identity*, Cambridge: Polity Press.

Spillman, L. (1997) *Nation and Commemoration: Creating National Identities in the United States and Australia*, Cambridge: Cambridge University Press.

Steinitz, S. (2006) 'Shalom Wien', *Profil*, 8, 86–94.

Stevenson, N. (2003) *Cultural Citizenship*, Maidenhead: Open University Press.

Stoisits, T. (2001) 'Meine Wurzeln waren schon immer da', in B. Coudenhove-Kalergi (ed.) *Meine Wurzeln sind anderswo: sterreichische Identit ten*, Vienna: Czernin Verlag.

Storper, M. (2001) 'Lived effects of the contemporary economy: globalization, inequality, and consumer society', in J. Comaroff and J.L. Comaroff (eds) *Millennial Capitalism and the Culture of Neoliberalism*, Durham: Duke University Press.

Strauss, C. and Quinn, N. (1997) *A Cognitive Theory of Cultural Meaning*, Cambridge: Cambridge University Press.

STS (2000) 'I bin aus Österreich', *STS & Band Live*, amadeo: 157 829–2 [CD].

Sully, M. (1990) *A Contemporary History of Austria*, London: Routledge.

Thaler, P. (2001) *The Ambivalence of Identity: The Austrian Experience of Nation-building in a Modern Society*, West Lafayette: Purdue University Press.

Turrini, P. (2001) *Ich liebe dieses Land*, Frankfurt: Suhrkamp.

Ulram, P.A. and Tributsch, S. (2004) *Kleine Nation mit Eigenschaften: ber das Verh ltnis der sterreicher zu sich selbst und ihren Nachbarn*, Vienna: Molden Verlag.

Vanderbeck, R.M. (2003) 'Youth, racism, and place in the Tony Martin affair', *Antipode*, 35 (2), 363–384.

Vertovec, S. (2000) *The Hindu Diaspora*, London: Routledge.

Wander, P. (2002) 'Introduction to the transaction edition', in H. Lefebvre *Everyday Life in the Modern World*, London/New York: Continuum.

Warrier, S. (1994) 'Gujarati Prajapatis in London: family roles and sociability networks', in R. Ballard (ed.) *Desh Pardesh: The South Asian Presence in Britain*, London: Hurst & Co.

Wassermann, H.P. (ed.) (2002) *Antisemitismus in sterreich nach 1945*, Innsbruck: Studien Verlag.

Weinzierl, E. (1997) *Zu Wenig Gerechte: sterreicher und die Judenverfolgung 1938—1945*, Graz: Styria.

Weiss, G. and Wodak, R. (eds) (2003) *Critical Discourse Analysis: Theory and Interdisciplinarity*, Basingstoke: Palgrave Macmillan.

Williams, R. (1977) *Marxism and Literature*, Oxford: Oxford University Press.

—— (1989 [1958]) 'Culture is ordinary', in R. Williams *Resources of Hope*, London/New York: Verso.

Wodak, R. (2000) 'Echt, anständig und ordentlich', in H-H. Scharsach (ed.) *Haider — sterreich und die rechte Versuchung*, Reinbek: Rowohlt.

www.groundswelluk.net/~fft.htm (2003) 'Beginners guide to gypsies and traveller issues', accessed 2 July.

www.orf.at (2004) 'Nichts als Ausnahmen?', 26 January.

—— (2004) 'Umfrage: Zuwanderer "mehr Belastung als Nutzen"', 16 September.

—— (2005) 'Grüne für Totalreform von Staatsbürgerschaftsrecht', 25 August.

—— (2005) 'Neues Staatsbürgerschaftsrecht abgesegnet', 6 December.

www.slamnet.org.uk/traveller_communities.html (2003) 'The traveller communities', accessed 18 July.

www.unhcr.ch (2005) 'Top story: asylum claims fall to lowest level for 16 years, says UNHCR', 2 March.

INDEX

Acton, T., 61
ageing populations, 155
agency, 11, 18, 64–5, 165–6, 168, 170;
    constrained by power structures, 73;
    culture relationship, 24, 25, 26; dual
    discursive competence, 94–5; ethnic
    boundaries, 22–3; forced migration,
    141; identity, 72, 91, 99; resistance to
    power structures, 114; the Righteous,
    168, 169; South Asians, 84, 96, 167;
    structuration theory, 27–9; structures
    of fear, 161; 'subjects-in-process', 71;
    tactics of resistance, 58; ways of
    seeing, 33
Ali, Monica, 92
Anderson, Benedict, 17
Anita and Me, 92
Anthias, Floya, 79, 95
anthropoemic/anthropophagic
    responses towards otherness, 102–3,
    108–11, 114, 116, 118–19, 124–5, 167
anti-Semitism, 116
anxiety: anxiety-controlling mechanisms,
    28; reactions towards migrants, 128,
    151, 157–8, 160, 163–4, 168
assimilation 101, 103; anthropophagic
    responses towards otherness, 102,
    108–9, 110, 111, 116, 118, 124;
    Travellers, 52, 54, 55

asylum seekers, 8, 127, 129, 130–1, 132,
    140; Austria, 108, 109, 118; Bauman
    on, 134, 159–60; ethnic majority
    response to, 151, 152–63; ethnic
    networks, 146–7; instrumental
    ethnicity, 146–51; numbers of, 136,
    154–5; otherness, 103; solidarity with,
    161–3; *see also* forced migration
Austria, 6–7, 101, 103, 104–26, 167;
    anthropoemic/anthropophagic
    responses towards otherness, 108–11;
    counter-hegemonic discourses,
    119–22; critical pluralism, 115–19;
    history of, 104–8; perceptions of
    national similarity, 111–13; popular
    music, 123–4
Austrian Freedom Party (FPÖ), 103, 113,
    121

Baert, P., 36, 41
Baldwin, James, 3
Ballard, Roger, 76, 77, 92, 93
Bancroft, Angus, 52, 56, 57, 67
Bangladeshis, 74, 75, 76, 77, 85–6
Barth, Fredrik, 22, 29
Barthes, Roland, 12
Bauman, Zygmunt:
    anthropoemic/anthropophagic
    responses to the stranger, 102, 108–9,